Enjoy Memories

St. Louis
SPORTS MEMORIES

Forgotten Teams and Moments from America's Best Sports Town

Ed Wheatley

Ed Wheatley

Copyright © 2022. Reedy Press, LLC
All rights reserved.

Reedy Press
PO Box 5131
St. Louis, MO 63139
www.reedypress.com

No part of this publication may be reproduced or transmitted in any form or by any means, electronic or mechanical, including photocopy, recording, or any information storage and retrieval system, without permission in writing from the publisher.

Permission may be sought directly from Reedy Press at the above mailing address or via our website at www.reedypress.com.

All images are courtesy of the author or believed to be in the public domain unless noted otherwise. For cover image credits, please refer to same images used within book pages.

Library of Congress Control Number: 2022937093

ISBN: 9781681064024

Design by Richard Roden

Printed in the United States

22 23 24 25 26   5 4 3 2 1

Contents

★ ★

A Sports Identity Is Formed VIII

Baseball
Four Major League Baseball Teams. 2
Baseball's Federal League Comes to Town. 6
Outside the MLB Chalk Lines 8
Into Extra Innings 13
Baseball for the Kids. 15
Five within a League of Their Own 17

Corkball
A St. Louis Original 20

Softball
These Browns Are Winners. 23
Women's Softball Takes Off 25

Basketball
Hoops Madness in St. Louis. 28
SLU's Home-Grown Boys Win It All 29
The Bombers Were First. 31
The Hawks Win It All and Leave 32
St. Louis's Greatest Basketball Player: Bob Pettit. 35
Was It a Good Trade or Not? Macauley, Russell, and the Ice Capades. . .36
The ABA Rolls into Town. 38
Near Perfection at the Arena: Bill Walton. 41
Wash U's Basketball Dynasty 43

Volleyball
A Volleyball Dynasty Too: Washington University 45

Bowling
The Pins Go Down in Bowling Town. 47
The Budweisers: Kings of the Lanes 49
St. Louis's Hall of Fame Quintet. 50
Still None Better: Team Budweiser 52

A Hall of Fame Comes, and a Hall of Fame Goes. 55
Strikes and Spares and Memories Galore 56

Football
The Forward Pass. 59
NFL 1-2-3-4 60
Not Many Stars on the All-Stars. 61
The Replacement Gunners 62
The Third Time's a Charm (Sort of): The Cardinals 64
Georgia Brings Them, and Stan Takes Them 70
Ka-Kaw and More: The XFL 76
An Arena Alternative: The AFL 78

Hockey
The Puck Dropped Long before the Blues: The Flyers 82
The Eagles Fly In 83
One More before the Blues: The Braves 84
The Blues Come Marching In 86
SLU Takes the Ice. 90
Slapshots 92

Soccer
Soccer Town. 94
The First Kicks to Greatness: Youth Soccer. 95
Soccer's Title Town. 97
The Hill's Fab Four. 101
Corner Kicks 103
St. Louis Soccer Goes Pro: Stars I 104
St. Louis Soccer Goes Pro: Stars II 106
Pele 109
Soccer Goes Indoors. 110
"Steamin'" in the Arena 111
Stormed 114
Ambushed 116
Same Name, Different League: The "New" Steamers 118
Leagues Come, Leagues Go 119

Golf
The Sport of Gentlemen Arrives. 122
The Big Boys Tee Off 124

The Day Golf Stopped: 9/11 128
Tee Shots 129

Tennis
Tennis Town. 133
Tennis's World Cup 134
He Really Was Good, Guys and Gals: Ted Drewes 135
The Start of a Town's Golden Age. 137
Momma Coaches St. Louis's Best: Jimmy Connors. 139
Champions Made at the Armory 141
From Richmond to Richmond Heights: Arthur Ashe. 142
Doubles Was His Game, Flach Was His Name. 144
The Golden Girls 145
Aces & Slims 148

Racing
They're Off and Running!. 151
Horses Weren't All That Raced: Auto Racing 152

Chess
Chess Is a Sport, and St. Louis Is Its Capital. 156

Professional Wrestling
Rasslin's Capital 159

Boxing
Knockouts 163

The Best Ever
Jackie Joyner-Kersee. 167

The Announcers
They Made Us Love the Game 169

We Cheered There
Sportsman's Park 172
The Old Barn. 174
St. Louis Public School Stadium. 175

Index 176

Track and Football
Star Bob Hayes
Courtesy of:
Wikimedia Commons

St. Louis Blues in the
1970 Stanley Cup Finals
Courtesy of:
Getty Images

VI | ST. LOUIS SPORTS MEMORIES

St. Louis Flyers 1946-47

1995-96 SCHEDULE

1886 St. Louis Maroons
Courtesy of: St. Louis Browns Historical Society & Fan Club

1958 World Champion St. Louis Hawks
Courtesy of: Getty Images

FORGOTTEN TEAMS AND MOMENTS FROM AMERICA'S BEST SPORTS TOWN | VII

A Sports Identity Is Formed

★ ★ ★ ★ ★ ★ ★ ★ ★ ★ ★ ★ ★ ★ ★ ★ ★ ★ ★ ★

Every American city, large or small, has a history built upon the identity of its people and their times. For centuries, St. Louis's identity was "the Gateway to the West." Due to their size and diversity, cities can take on many different identities over time. St. Louis first became a river town and then a beer town with the likes of the Anheuser-Busch, Falstaff, Griesedieck, and Stag breweries. At one time, with its multiple Chrysler, Ford, and General Motors plants, St. Louis was a leader in the auto industry, ranking second only to Detroit in automobile production. From the highways to the skyways and outer space, St. Louis led America's space race with the Mercury, Gemini, and Space Lab programs built by McDonnell Aircraft, which also ruled the skies as a world leader in military aircraft with their Phantom, Eagle, Harrier, and Hornet jets.

Throughout these years of transition and development, there evolved a common presence within every American city: sports. By the mid-1800s, sporting events were being held in every American town. Sports became entertainment that brought people together at a time when there were no movie theatres, television sets, or video games. It was a time when communities could unite through competition, both locally and against other towns. While many cities have had success in the sports world, St. Louis evolved as one of the most diverse and successful athletic towns in America, led by many of the greatest personalities across numerous sports.

Each of St. Louis's major professional teams has hoisted its sport's championship trophies. So, too, have lesser teams within the professional and college ranks that called the St. Louis region home. The town's history goes beyond just winning championships. Throughout the region's rich history, there is so much more to explore and relive than just these wins.

Sports can provide a commentary on the social issues that confront a city and the nation. A St. Louis baseball team, at the time the most southern in the major leagues, was the first to field two African American ballplayers as the third and fourth players to cross major-league baseball's color line. St. Louis had the first female owner of a major-league baseball team as well as the first woman owner in the NFL who also moved her team to town . . . and no, she wasn't a Ram. St. Louis was also at the forefront in the organization of women's bowling. A future tennis star would leave his segregated hometown and come to St. Louis to master his game in an open and accepting environment during the civil unrest of the 1960s. Another star's mother began training him at the age of two to be not only St. Louis's best, but the best in the world.

Teams have come and gone, but let's not forget them. Today, few fans can recite all four MLB teams or the four NFL teams that called St. Louis home. The Blues weren't the town's first NHL team, and the Hawks weren't its first NBA team.

St. Louis colleges dominated one sport with 31 national titles over a 58-year span. Other schools would have double-digit national championships in other sports as well.

One of the greatest players in NBA history spent his entire career with a St. Louis franchise and still ranks at the top of many of the sport's statistical categories. Another athlete is known for frozen custard, yet he was one of the best at his game. Three of the most prestigious trophies in sports are named after St. Louisans—one in golf, one in soccer, and one in tennis. As time passes, let us not forget these individuals, their teams, or their moments as new histories and memories continue to be made.

There are instances when many major sports have recognized St. Louis as their capital. Bowling, soccer, wrestling, and even chess are just a few examples. It's more than just winning; it is the history and tradition that evolved within the city.

The greatness of St. Louis's sports history is that the city has never been branded as a one-dimensional sports town. The diversity of sports and their defining moments are etched on fields, in stadiums, and within the walls of arenas and clubs across this town. This history consists not only of professional experiences, but also includes the accomplishments of boys and girls, men and women, and people of all ages, colors, and creeds. Sports help define this river city and have been part of its legacy.

While this is not a complete narrative of the history of St. Louis athletes and competition, it is representative of the diversity of the city's experience and prominence across the world of sports. Not only do the town's sports franchises have a winning edge, they have an edge due to their fan base. Throughout this narrative, it's noted time and again how St. Louis teams led their leagues in attendance. Part of that is due to each team's success, but it is also attributable to the members of the media who convey the excitement of the games to their audience.

It's easy to cheer when you are watching winning teams comprised of hall of famers, but many special moments are made by players who will never set foot into a hall of fame. Even though backup catcher Glen Brummer will never be a Hall of Famer, he helped spark the 1982 Cardinals to the pennant by stealing home, and his is a special St. Louis sports moment that will be cherished by the fans. The same with Doug Wickenheiser's special Monday night or Mel Gray's phantom catch. And what about the St. Louis Browns, a team that lost 1,000 more games than they won? Today they still have a very active fan club even though they haven't played in 69 seasons. It's the same for football's not-very-good Big Red team. Fans still rally around them and all of the St. Louis teams of the past. Why? It's because of the many special moments from their games that entertained us and became cherished memories to us all. So let's all appreciate them and keep going to the next game, because you never know what memory or moment you might see.

ST. LOUIS SPORTS MEMORIES

Baseball

KHOURY LEAGUE SINCE 1936 YOUTH BASEBALL, SOFTBALL & SOCCER

St. Louis BROWNS

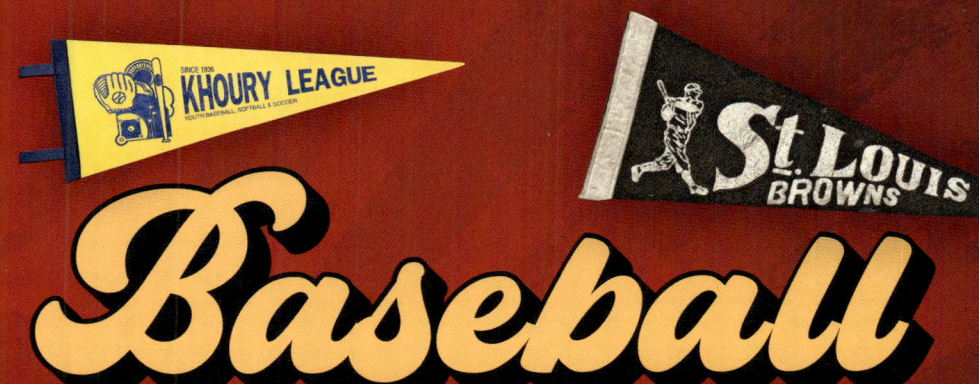

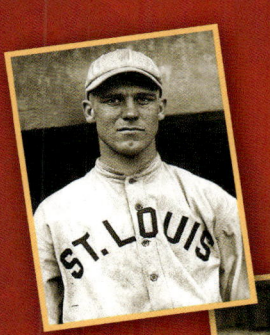

1902 St. Louis Browns
Courtesy of: St. Louis Browns Historical Society & Fan Club

George Sisler
Courtesy of: St. Louis Browns Historical Society & Fan Club

St. Louis Terriers player sliding into third base
Courtesy of: Missouri History Museum, St. Louis

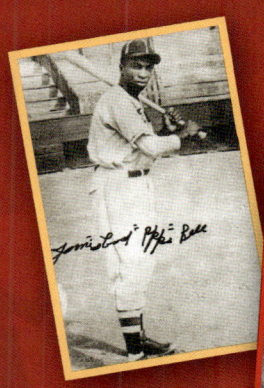

St. Louis CARDINALS

James "Cool Papa" Bell
Courtesy of: Missouri History Museum, St. Louis

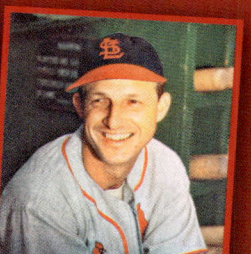

Satchel Paige
Courtesy of: St. Louis Browns Historical Society & Fan Club

Stan Musial
Courtesy of: Wikimedia Commons

Four Major League Baseball Teams

★ ★

When one thinks of St. Louis sports greatness, baseball immediately pops to the top of the list. Bob Costas and others have called St. Louis the "best baseball town in America." After all, the Cardinals' 11 World Championships are second only to the New York Yankees. But that history is not just about the Cardinals. Baseball in St. Louis dates back to July 9, 1860, a year before the Civil War, when the Cyclones played the Morning Stars at Fairgrounds Park in the city's first game played under the organized national rules of the game.

Few fans today realize that since the National League first began play in 1876, there have been 4 different Major League teams that have called St. Louis home. The Brown Stockings joined the National League in 1876, in its inaugural season, and played for just two years before being terminated for gambling issues. In 1885, the St. Louis Maroons were invited to join the National League to compete against the success of a new Brown Stockings team playing in the American Association (1882–1891) under owner Chris Von der Ahe. The American Association was also known as the "beer and whiskey league" because, unlike the National League, they allowed alcohol and Sunday games. While the Brown Stockings garnered four straight American Association championship titles beginning in 1885, the Maroons faltered financially and folded in

1876 St. Louis Brown Stockings
Courtesy of: Wikimedia Commons

1886. In 1892, a third St. Louis team was brought into the National League when that league's leaders decided that if they couldn't compete against Von der Ahe's team they might as well bring them into the National League—and that's just what they did.

Today's Cardinals trace their franchise lineage all the way back to Von der Ahe's 1892 entry. With a shortened name, they joined the League as the St. Louis Browns. The team used that title until 1899, when they became the Perfectos. A year later they adopted a new name and forever became the Cardinals.

1899 St. Louis Perfectos
Courtesy of: Library of Congress

By 1902, St. Louis was the nation's fourth-largest city, and baseball was the country's biggest form of entertainment. The American League, which had formed a year earlier in 1901, decided to move its Milwaukee Brewers club to St. Louis and give its baseball fans the luxury of having a team in each league. The new American League team adopted the name "Browns" and kept it until they left town to become the Baltimore Orioles in 1954. Losing nearly 1,000 more games than they won, the Browns became baseball's first loveable losers, and were known by the slogan "first in beer, first in shoes, and last in the American League."

Both the Browns and the Cardinals have had many memorable and historic moments documented in countless books and films. In 1944, they each won their league's pennant and faced each other in that year's World Series. It truly was the year that baseball fans sang the song, "Meet Me in St. Louie, Louie," but instead of meeting at the fair, they met at Sportsman's Park.

Many baseball historians attribute the Cardinals' greatness to the genius and vision of Branch Rickey. Ironically, Rickey began his lengthy

Branch Rickey
Courtesy of: St. Louis Browns
Historical Society & Fan Club

baseball career with the American League Browns and left over his desire to create what would become baseball's first farm system. The Browns owner, Phillip Ball, didn't want to spend the money on the investment. The Cardinals new owner, Sam Breadon, did, so Rickey soon joined the Redbirds. The rest is history—or should we say pennants? Rickey's farm system developed the great players that led to the Cardinals' pennants in 1926, 1928, 1930, 1931, 1934, 1942, 1943, 1944, and 1946; only to leave Brownie fans wishing he had remained a Brown.

Outside the great players and stories of both teams, there are unique pieces of baseball lore and history to remember. Long before inter-league play began in 1997, St. Louis baseball fans got to see the best of both the American and National League players coming to town. The two teams shared the same stadium (Sportsman's Park) from 1920 to 1953. The Cardinals team history included the Gashouse Gang, the Swifties, the El Birdos, and Whitey Ball. They've had Rogers Hornsby, Dizzy Dean, and Ducky Medwick's Triple Crown. Then came Stan "the Man" Musial hitting 5 homers in a day and Lou Brock setting base-stealing records, while Gibson threw K's in the World Series. And don't forget Ozzie's flips, Big Mac's smashes, the Waino/Molina duo, and Albert playing like no other had played before. These are just a few of the names and moments that make Cardinal history so great. Despite having George Sisler, one of the greatest hitters in baseball history in their lineup, the

4 | ST. LOUIS SPORTS MEMORIES

Browns are too often known for using a one-armed player named Pete Gray in 1945, the day in 1951 when 3' 7" Eddie Gaedel stepped up to the plate, or five days later when fans in the grandstands made the decisions and managed the Browns for a game. By the way, the Browns won that latter game—maybe they should have used the fans to manage more often.

There is, however, one very special moment in Browns history that is not given the attention it deserves and is overlooked in most history books. The Browns were the first team to field two African American players and it occurred just a few months after Jackie Robinson crossed baseball's color line and only days after Larry Doby became the second African American to make it to the big leagues with the Indians. The St. Louis Browns, playing in what was at the time the southernmost city in all of baseball, actually fielded the third and fourth African American players to make it to the majors when Hank Thompson took the field on July 17, 1947, and Willard Brown on July 19, 1947, and then took the field together on July 20, 1947. It would be seven more years before the Cardinals' first African American player, Tom Alston, would suit up in April 1954, and 12 years before the Boston Red Sox would be MLB's last team to integrate in 1959.

Willard Brown and Hank Thompson
Courtesy of: St. Louis Browns Historical Society & Fan Club

Staffed with a combined 64 Hall of Famers and other great players and squads, these four teams have provided an unrivaled history of baseball memories and a fan base that easily earns St. Louis recognition as the "best baseball town in America." But that reputation was not built solely on its Major League presence.

Baseball's Federal League Comes to Town

The Federal League was formed in 1913 as a revolt against MLB's reserve clause, which allowed teams to retain exclusive rights to players even after their contracts expired. The Federal League only played the 1914 and 1915 seasons, but when the first pitch was thrown in the inaugural season of 1914, the league featured eight teams, including a team from St. Louis named the Terriers. Almost five decades before former Cardinal Curt Flood would challenge the rules that would lead to today's free agency, the Federal League began recruiting (white) players from other teams and was soon branded an "outlaw league."

Sporting royal blue and white uniforms and playing in Handlan's Park Grounds on the southeast corner of Grand and Laclede Avenues (today's Saint Louis University campus), the St. Louis Terriers had only moderate success during their short tenure. In 1914, they finished dead last, 25 games behind the champion Indianapolis Hoosiers. The most noted player on the 1914 Terriers team was Mordecai "Three Finger" Brown, who had been lured from the National League's Cincinnati Reds. In a way, it was a homecoming for Brown, as he had begun his Hall of Fame career with the St. Louis Cardinals, playing with the team in the 1903 season before heading off to fame with the Chicago Cubs between 1904 and 1912.

In the second and final Federal League season, the Terriers showed marked improvement. They contended for the pennant down to the last game of the season before finishing in second place with an 87–67 (.565) record. They finished just one-one thousandth of a percentage point behind the champion Chicago Whales, who posted an 86–66 record (.566), having played two fewer games. The Terriers' change in fortune was due to the experienced players who were signed for the 1915 season—especially Belleville, Illinois's Bob Groom, future Hall of Famer Eddie Plank, and Johnny Tobin. They would each leave their marks on St. Louis's baseball history, most notably as members of the American League's St. Louis Browns. While pitching for the Terriers, Plank won his 300th game on September 14, 1915, making him the first of only six left-handed pitchers to do so.

Eddie Plank
Courtesy of: Library of Congress

This St. Louis Browns connection began with the Terriers' owner and local St. Louis ice magnate Philip Ball. He would in time shape the future of both of the city's major league teams—the Browns and Cardinals. The Federal League challenged MLB's labor stranglehold in an antitrust suit after the 1914 season. The suit fell before the bench of Judge Kenesaw Mountain Landis, who would soon become the first commissioner of baseball. The suit dragged on throughout the 1915 season, after which MLB owners put this outlaw league and its lawsuit to bed by buying out four Federal League teams (Brooklyn, Buffalo, Newark, and Pittsburgh). They also allowed two Federal League owners to purchase struggling MLB teams and merge their Federal League teams with their purchased teams. The Terriers' owners bought the American League's St. Louis Browns, and Chicago Whales owner Charles Weeghman bought the Chicago Cubs. As previously noted, Ball's ownership of the St. Louis American League team would have a significant impact on the city's two major league teams, as his feud with Branch Rickey over the development of the farm system doomed the Browns and set the stage for the Cardinals' future success. In the end, the buyouts brought an end to the Federal League and the last real attempt to form a third major league—that is, at least a league for white players.

Outside the MLB Chalk Lines

★ ★

St. Louis's acclaimed baseball history and fan base are not limited to the major leagues. There is a rich history written both by those who could not cross the major-league color line and those who played in a "renegade league" that challenged the structure of the big leagues. While the greatness of the Negro Leagues has been heralded in recent decades through stories about the Kansas City Monarchs or the Homestead Grays, St. Louis lays claim to one of the greatest Negro League franchises of all time with the history of the Giants (1906–1921)/Stars (1922–1931).

How good were these teams? Five players from the two teams have been enshrined in Cooperstown's Hall of Fame (James "Cool Papa" Bell, Oscar Charleston, James "Biz" Mackey, George "Mule" Suttles, and Willie Wells). The Stars won 3 pennants in the 12 years of the Negro National League's (NNL's) existence before it folded due to the Great Depression after the 1931 season.

The St. Louis Giants had been around for nearly a decade, playing in independent leagues in and around the area before joining the NNL when it was formed in Kansas City in 1920. Prior to joining the NNL, they played most of their games against top area white teams, including exhibition games with the St. Louis Cardinals. The

St. Louis Giants Team Photo
Courtesy of: Missouri History Museum, St. Louis

Giants played at different parks around the St. Louis area before settling into Giants Park at Broadway and Clarence Avenues.

The Giants were led by Charles Mills, an African American businessman who should be recognized as the father of St. Louis Negro League baseball. He led the Giants through independent league play from 1909 to 1921, struggling to keep the team financially sound while fielding a formidable group of players. At the beginning of the 1920s, the Giants were a so-so team that kept adding talent, including the franchise's biggest star, Hall of Famer Oscar Charleston. In their first year in the new eight-team league, the Giants finished sixth with a record of 25-32. In 1921, the team finished in second place with a 42-30 record, as the Chicago American Giants repeated as champions. But improvement on the field did not necessarily mean financial improvement for Mills and his team. Behind the scenes there was a battle over the team's leadership and direction under Mills' ownership that had been going on for years. Just as MLB would force Bill Veeck to sell the Browns 33 years later, the NNL powers successfully pushed Mills out after the 1921 season.

Dr. Samuel Shepard and Richard Kent took over the franchise in April 1922, and renamed the team the Stars. They also built a 10,000 seat stadium exclusively for the Stars at Compton and Market Streets that today is the baseball field of Harris-Stowe University. They placed the team in the hands of manager Jim "Candy" Taylor and went about putting together a championship-caliber team with the likes of center fielder "Cool Papa" Bell, shortstop Willie Wells, first baseman Mule Suttles, catcher Quincy Trouppe, and

Stars Park
Courtesy of: Missouri History Museum, St. Louis

St. Louis Stars Team Photo
Courtesy of: Missouri History Museum,
St. Louis

pitcher Ted Trent. Suttles, who swung a 50-ounce bat, would wind up as the all-time Negro League home run king.

What a town of champions St. Louis had become—while the St. Louis Cardinals were winning pennants in 1926, 1928, 1930, and 1931, the Stars took the NNL pennant in 1928, 1930, and 1931. Off the field, the financial hardships of the Great Depression were hitting the league hard. In 1931, the Stars' pennant win was by default, as they were awarded the championship when the league disbanded partway through the season. The Stars soon folded with the rest of the league.

For the record, the 1931 demise of the Stars and the NNL was not the complete end of Negro League play across the country or in St. Louis. It did, however, mark the high point of Negro League affiliation in St. Louis. As in the early history of MLB, there were many offshoots and iterations of Negro League baseball. The Eastern Colored League operated from 1923 to 1928. The American Negro League played a single season in 1929, and the East–West League and Negro Southern League each played a single season in 1932. Two other ventures had longer lifespans: a second version of the Negro National League lasted from 1933 to 1948, and the Negro American League operated from 1937 to 1960.

A team named the St. Louis Stars played off and on across different leagues from 1937 to 1943. As one of the eight teams playing in the 1937 inaugural season of the Negro American League, the Stars finished dead last, 27 games behind the Kansas City Monarchs with a record of 4 wins and 27 losses. The team ceased play in 1938, but had a revival in 1939 when the Indianapolis ABCs moved to St. Louis and won the second-half title in the League's split-season format before losing to the mighty Kansas City Monarchs 3 games to 2 in the championship playoff. Always fighting to stay afloat financially, the Stars developed a co-hosting relationship in 1940 and 1941 with New Orleans under the moniker St. Louis–New Orleans Stars. The team disbanded in 1942, but the St. Louis team co-hosted with a club from Harrisburg, Pennsylvania, in 1943. This NNL team was known as the Harrisburg–St. Louis Stars. It lasted only until July of that season, dropping out of the league in favor of a more lucrative barnstorming tour with Dizzy Dean's All-Stars or Satchel Paige's various teams.

The Negro Leagues entertained their fans with an exciting brand of baseball, but they could not overcome the financial pressures of the times and a segregated world. Impacted by white booking agents who controlled gate revenues, the Negro League teams never achieved the necessary financial stability to fully survive the hardships of the Depression followed by the impact of World War II. Most Negro League activities folded after the 1947 integration of baseball, as black players took advantage of new opportunities. By 1950, all that really remained of organized Negro League baseball was barnstorming teams that traversed the country playing games here and there. While baseball's "color line" had been crossed and the door was open, the progression of African American players to the majors remained slow. By the end of the 1949 MLB season and three seasons after Jackie Robinson's debut on April 15, 1947, only 11 African American players had made it to the major leagues. Those 11 players were on just 4 of the league's 16 teams, and two of them were on the St. Louis Browns: Willard Brown and Hank Thompson. Both by hosting a successful Negro League team and by fielding the third and fourth African American players in the major leagues, St. Louis truly was a progressive leader in the world of baseball.

St. Louis Negro League Baseball Stats

YEAR	TEAM	LG	G	W	L	TIES	W-L%	FINISH
1920	St. Louis Giants	NNL	72	32	40	0	0.444	6th of 8
1921	St. Louis Giants	NNL	75	43	31	1	0.581	3rd of 8
1922	St. Louis Stars	NNL	62	26	36	0	0.419	5th of 8
1923	St. Louis Stars	NNL	72	29	43	0	0.403	10th of 8
1924	St. Louis Stars	NNL	84	43	41	0	0.512	4th of 9
1925	St. Louis Stars	NNL	91	59	30	2	0.663	2nd of 8
1926	St. Louis Stars	NNL	98	61	35	2	0.635	3rd of 8
1927	St. Louis Stars	NNL	99	62	37	0	0.626	2nd of 8
1928	St. Louis Stars	NNL	89	63	26	0	0.708	1st of 8
1929	St. Louis Stars	NNL	91	56	34	1	0.622	2nd of 7
1930	St. Louis Stars	NNL	95	69	25	1	0.734	1st of 9
1931	St. Louis Stars	NNL	48	37	10	1	0.787	1st of 6
	TOTAL	NNL	976	580	388	8	0.594	
1937	St. Louis Stars	NAL	37	5	32	0	0.135	8th of 8
1938	Indianapolis ABCs	NAL	37	17	20	0	0.459	4th of 7
1939	St. Louis Stars	NAL	36	15	20	1	0.429	6th of 7
1940	St. Louis-New Orleans Stars	NAL	41	20	19	2	0.513	4th of 7
1941	St. Louis-New Orleans Stars	NAL	37	16	19	2	0.457	3rd of 6
1943	Harrisburg Stars	NN2	16	8	8	0	0.5	3rd of 7

Into Extra Innings

⭐ Between 1882 and 1891, baseball's American Association Champion would play the National League's Champion for what was considered baseball's World Championship. Chris Von der Ahe's 1886 St. Louis Browns (shortened from Brown Stockings) were the only American Association team that would capture a World Championship win in the series when they defeated the National League's Chicago White Stockings that year. Interestingly, this series is looked upon as the start of one of today's greatest baseball rivalries, between the Cardinals and Cubs. By 1902, the White Stockings would begin being called the Cubs, and in 1892, the Browns would join the National League, changing their name to the Cardinals in 1900.

⭐ In 1911, Helene Britton (née Robison) inherited the St. Louis Cardinals upon her uncle's death and became the first female owner of a Major League team. She was very active in running the team and is credited for refusing substantial offers to sell a top prospect to pay off some revenue shortfalls. That prospect's name was Rogers Hornsby, and he became one of the franchise's greatest players.

Helene Britton
Courtesy of: Missouri History Museum, St. Louis

⭐ When looking across the histories of professional baseball, basketball, football, and hockey, it is interesting to note that in 1922, the St. Louis Browns' George Sisler won the first-ever MLB Most Valuable Player Award, and 34 seasons later during the 1955–56 season, Bob Pettit of the St. Louis Hawks won the first ever NBA Most Valuable Player Award.

⭐ Speaking of MVPs, more Cardinal players have won the award than any other team. 16 Cardinals have taken it home, which is four more than the Dodgers' and Yankees' 12 players. The Yankees players in total

FORGOTTEN TEAMS AND MOMENTS FROM AMERICA'S BEST SPORTS TOWN | 13

have won it 21 times to the Cardinals 20. The Cardinals winners are Rogers Hornsby (1924), Bob O'Farrell (1926), Jim Bottomley (1928), Frankie Frisch (1931), Dizzy Dean (1934), Joe Medwick (1937), Mort Cooper (1942), Stan Musial (1943, 1946, 1948), Marty Marion (1944), Ken Boyer (1964), Bob Gibson (1968), Orlando Cepeda (1967), Joe Torre (1971), Keith Hernandez (1979), Willie McGee (1985), and Albert Pujols (2005, 2008, 2009).

⭐ There have been three players who grew up in St. Louis who also won MLB's MVP award, Yogi Berra (1951, 1954, and 1955) and the two Howards, Elston (1962) and Ryan (2006).

⭐ Roy Sievers of the St. Louis Browns won the first-ever American League Rookie of the Year Award in 1949. Fans only remember the Browns as loveable losers, yet they had the game's first MVP and first American League Rookie of the Year—not too shabby!

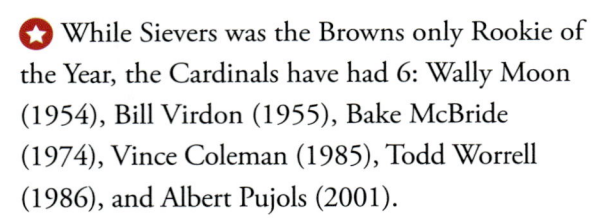

⭐ While Sievers was the Browns only Rookie of the Year, the Cardinals have had 6: Wally Moon (1954), Bill Virdon (1955), Bake McBride (1974), Vince Coleman (1985), Todd Worrell (1986), and Albert Pujols (2001).

Roy Sievers
Courtesy of: St. Louis Browns Historical Society & Fan Club

⭐ During the late 1940s and early 1950s, more men (14) played in the Major Leagues from one St. Louis high school than from any other high school in the country. That school? St. Louis Beaumont High School, located at Natural Bridge and Vandeventer on the site of the St. Louis Cardinals' former stadium, Robison Field. It was always said there must have been some very special baseball magic left on that site that turned Beaumont into a "baseball factory." In recent years, Lafayette High School has produced six MLB players, including Philadelphia's MVP Ryan Howard and Cardinals World Series hero David Freese.

Baseball for the Kids

Today, many baseball fans neither remember nor appreciate the impact that one man from the Gateway City has had on youth baseball across the nation and around the world. His name was George Khoury. He founded the George Khoury Association of Baseball Leagues, or simply the Khoury League, in St. Louis in 1934. The Khoury League is the longest-operating youth program in America, and it was created in St. Louis, where it is still headquartered.

Since its creation, the Khoury League has touched millions of kids by sponsoring T-ball, baseball, and softball for kids ages four and up in a structure that allows

George Khoury and the kids
Courtesy of: Khoury League Archives

them to advance in a progressive format with different-sized balls and field dimensions, thus allowing young ballplayers to grow into the game as they mature. How many former little leaguers remember the changing size of the baseball as they moved up from the Atom to Bantam to Midget divisions?

Khoury was born in St. Louis in 1900 to parents who had emigrated from Lebanon. He grew up suffering through the poverty and the hardships of the Great Depression before finding success in the printing business. His struggles and eventual financial success motivated him to help others, especially the children in the community. Spurred by his wife Dorothy's suggestion that he organize a baseball club for their three sons and their friends, Khoury started a league that brought kids together to play baseball as a productive way to spend their free time and thus stay out of trouble.

The association began play in St. Louis in 1936. The first games were played on Mother's Day in Forest Park in honor of Khoury's wife. The association was immediately popular and grew quickly, especially after World War II, with organizations expanding across the country and internationally. The Cardinals and Browns sponsored fundraising efforts for the Khoury League and hosted the league's annual all-star game at Sportsman's Park. What a special memory it was for little league ballplayers to take the field where their heroes played and then get that memorable team photo with Sportsman's Park's huge scoreboard in the background along with certificates for their scrapbooks.

Khoury League All-Stars
Courtesy of: Khoury League Archives

The Khoury League continued to grow in popularity. Local newspapers like the *Post-Dispatch* provided regular coverage of each week's games, and television station KPLR, which had begun broadcasting in 1959, televised Khoury League games across the city as it built up its programming schedule. In 1958, girls were finally brought into the fold as softball was introduced into the Khoury League.

Many major league ballplayers and umpires developed their early baseball skills on Khoury League teams across the region and would go on to star in high school before signing their pro contracts. Most notable are Frank Bauman (St. Louis—Central High School), Homer Bush (East St. Louis—East St. Louis High School), Dal Maxvill (Granite City—Granite City High School), Mike Shannon (St. Louis—CBC High School), and Earl Weaver (St. Louis—Beaumont High School). Major league umpire Dave Phillips (Jennings High School) also got his start playing and learning the game in the Khoury League.

The Khoury League helped supply many local high schools with good baseball talent and even provided the nucleus of the region's only collegiate championship when Coach Ric Lessman's Meramec team won the National Junior College title in 1974.

Five within a League of Their Own

★ ★

There are few sports fans today that have not seen the 1992 movie *A League of Their Own* starring Tom Hanks and Madonna. It captured the story of the All-American Girls Professional Baseball League (AAGPBL) that was formed in 1943 by Philip K. Wrigley, of candy and chewing-gum fame, who also happened to also own the Chicago Cubs. The league, originally known as the All-American Girls Softball League, was created to fill the entertainment void left when many major- and minor-league (male) players were off fighting in World War II. Over time, the league transitioned from softball to baseball. Throughout the 12-year history of the league, the rules were gradually modified to more closely resemble baseball. Even after the war's end it remained popular and continued another decade before disbanding in 1954.

The league would have as many as 10 teams during its tenure, and all were located in the upper Midwest. St. Louis would never host a team. While the Springfield, Illinois, Sallies (1948) were the closest team to St. Louis, five women from the area did play in the league. These five women were good athletes and playing softball when scouted in the area. A few had included baseball in their résumés. They were:

⭐ Erma Bergmann, a pitcher and outfielder from St. Louis City, played for the Muskegon Lassies (1946–47), the Springfield Sallies (1948), the Racine Belles (1949–50), and the Battle Creek Belles (1951). Erma initially began pitching underhand and through the leagues evolution became one of the few hurlers to pitch all three styles as she transitioned to full sidearm in 1947 and then

FORGOTTEN TEAMS AND MOMENTS FROM AMERICA'S BEST SPORTS TOWN | 17

to overhand in 1948. Erma pitched a no-hitter in 1947. As a side note, after leaving baseball Erma became the first commissioned policewoman in the city of St. Louis.

⭐ Audrey "Kiss" Kissel from St. Louis City played for the Minneapolis Millerettes in 1944. Nicknamed "Kiss" by her teammates and "pigtails" by the press for the way she wore her hair, Kissel played second base for just one season before giving up baseball to marry her boyfriend, whom she earlier thought she had lost in action in WWII. When he was found, she left baseball and joined him before what would have been her second season.

⭐ Raised in Florissant, Rita "Slats" Meyers played for the Peoria Redwings (1946–1949). She was nicknamed "Slats" because she was a shortstop whose stature resembled that of Cardinal great Marty Marion. Sometimes Rita would also pitch, and she threw a no-hitter in 1947 despite her team losing the game 1-0. In 1948, Rita was the league's RBI champion.

⭐ Edna Frank was a catcher from St. Louis. She played 16 games with the Minneapolis Millerettes in 1944 before being traded to the Racine Belles. Edna was not happy about the trade, and instead of reporting to Racine, she joined the Navy in support of the war effort and to see the world.

⭐ Barb Hoffman of Belleville, Illinois, played for the South Bend Blue Sox (1951–52) and is the lone surviving player from St. Louis. Playing second and third base, Barb helped her team win their first AAGPBL title in 1951. The next year she was an all-star and even homered in the all-star game but left the team with several other players due to a disagreement with the team's manager.

18 | ST. LOUIS SPORTS MEMORIES

Corkball

Playing corkball in the alleys and schoolyards of St. Louis.
Courtesy of: Newspaper.com

A St. Louis Original

★ ★ ★ ★ ★ ★ ★ ★ ★ ★ ★ ★ ★ ★ ★ ★ ★ ★ ★ ★

In the epicurean world of dining, toasted ravioli is one of St. Louis's classic culinary treats and, as the saying goes, "a St. Louis original." In a spinoff of baseball, corkball was definitely St. Louis's sporting treat to the world. As people think back to their youth, how many recall seeing the game's caged courts throughout the city?

Like the many tales of where toasted ravioli was first unveiled, there are multiple versions of corkball's origin, and they all center on St. Louis. One thing is for sure: the rest of the nation learned of the game from St. Louis servicemen during their deployments on land and at sea during WWII and the Korean Conflict. There is even the story about a local St. Louisan by the name of Yogi Berra teaching his Yankee teammates how to play the game right in Yankee Stadium.

One story has the game being first played at Mueller's, a boardinghouse and saloon on the corner of Grand and Greer on the north side of town. Chris Von der Ahe, who happened to have owned the American Association Brown Stockings, also owned Mueller's in 1890. It was one of his players who, while enjoying the refreshments, pulled the bung out of the beer keg, made it into the shape of a ball, and began pitching it to a teammate who tried hitting it with a broomstick. Another player joined as a fielder, and another as a catcher. And from there, it became the simple game that grew across the region and the world.

The beauty of the game is that it can be played almost anywhere. It can be played in streets or alleys and even in confined areas indoors. As a measure to avoid secondary damage to the surroundings as the game became more popular, corkball cages were erected throughout the town, most notably within and outside taverns.

This St. Louis original is simple in design. Pitchers throw whatever type or speed of pitch they wish to a hitter—generally fast. A hitter is allowed one swinging strike or two called strikes for an out. Five called balls is a walk. Foul balls and any caught fly balls are outs, and there are three outs in an inning. The distance of a batter's hit ball, if not caught for an out, determines the type of hit. Playing fields are traditionally 30 feet wide and 250 feet long, with different variations of distances agreed upon in advance to determine if a hit is a single, double, triple, or home run. The twist is that there are no runners in the game. Baserunners are tracked on paper and adjusted by subsequent at bats.

With the new sport's success, corkball equipment began being produced and sold solely for this unique game. St. Louis–based Rawlings and Markwort Sporting Goods became the leading suppliers. The game uses a miniature 2-inch, 1.6-ounce stitched ball resembling a miniature baseball. The bat can be the length of a regular baseball bat, but the barrel can only be 1.5 inches in diameter.

While the number of taverns and their cages may have diminished with suburban migration, Corkball remains popular today with many leagues still in existence across the area. There have been spinoffs of this simple game played by young and old alike over the years called "Indian Ball" and "Fuzz-ball," and even a game using bottle caps instead of a ball, all of which continue to keep the excitement of swinging for the fences alive.

FORGOTTEN TEAMS AND MOMENTS FROM AMERICA'S BEST SPORTS TOWN

Softball

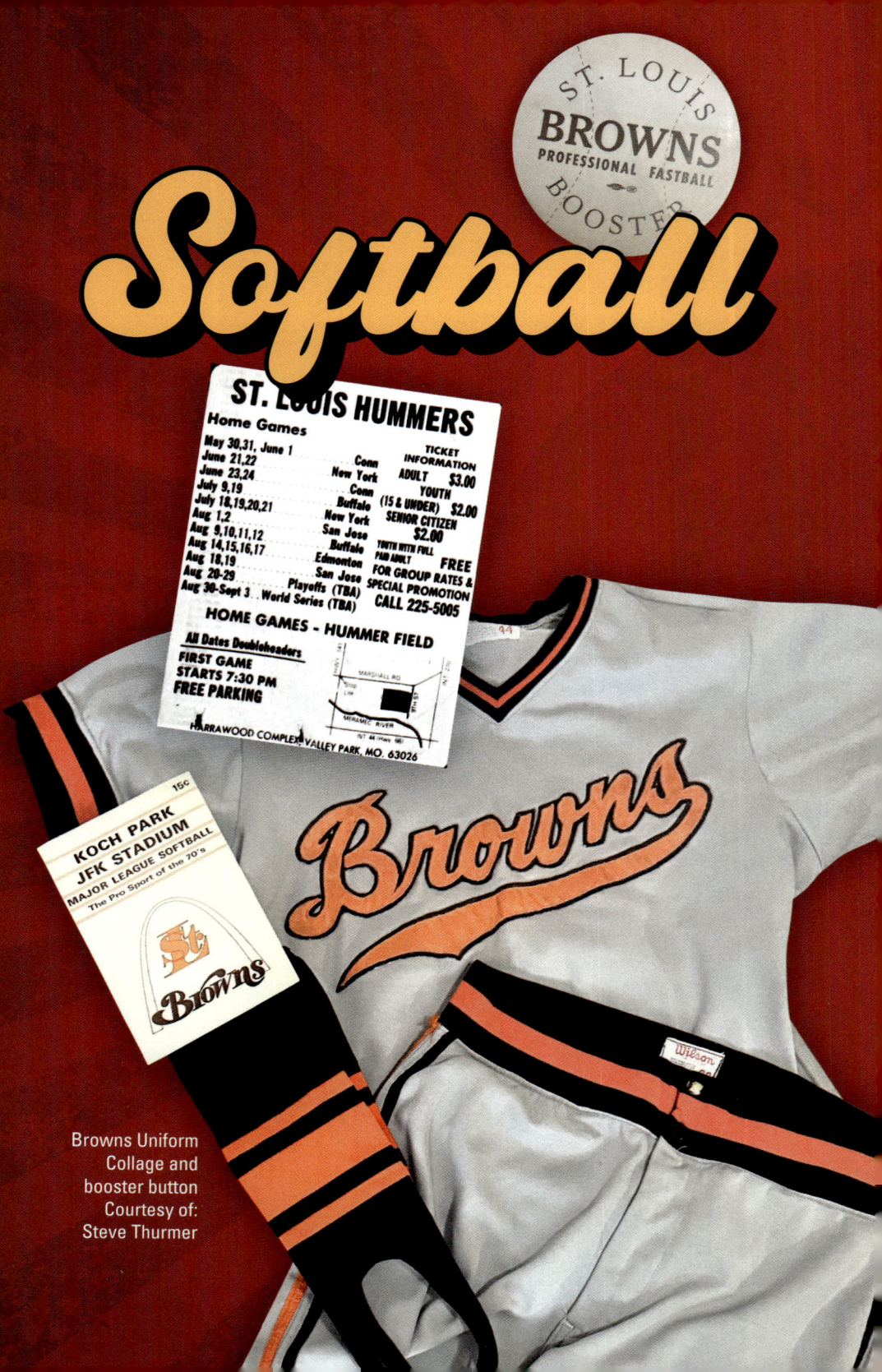

ST. LOUIS BROWNS PROFESSIONAL FASTBALL BOOSTER

ST. LOUIS HUMMERS
Home Games

May 30,31, June 1	Conn
June 21,22	New York
June 23,24	Conn
July 9,19	Buffalo
July 18,19,20,21	New York
Aug. 1,2	San Jose
Aug. 9,10,11,12	Buffalo
Aug. 14,15,16,17	Edmonton
Aug. 18,19	San Jose
Aug. 20-29	Playoffs (TBA)
Aug. 30-Sept 3	World Series (TBA)

TICKET INFORMATION
ADULT $3.00
YOUTH (15 & UNDER) $2.00
SENIOR CITIZEN $2.00
YOUTH WITH FULL PAID ADULT FREE
FOR GROUP RATES & SPECIAL PROMOTION CALL 225-5005

HOME GAMES - HUMMER FIELD
All Dates Doubleheaders
FIRST GAME STARTS 7:30 PM
FREE PARKING

HARRAWOOD COMPLEX VALLEY PARK, MO. 63026

15¢

KOCH PARK
JFK STADIUM
MAJOR LEAGUE SOFTBALL
The Pro Sport of the 70's

St Browns

Browns Uniform Collage and booster button Courtesy of: Steve Thurmer

These Browns Are Winners

★ ★ ★ ★ ★ ★ ★ ★ ★ ★ ★ ★ ★ ★ ★ ★ ★ ★ ★ ★

Back in the summer of 1973, Major League Softball Inc. (MLSI) was formed as a fast-pitch professional softball league across North America. Besides teams from the United States, there were teams in Montreal and Toronto. For the league's other cities, you needed a scorecard. Many teams came and went during the league's lone season. The lack of fans and the lack of money weighed heavy on a league that required lengthy travel.

Browns Team Photo
(Top Row L-R): Hummel–press; Vowell–of; Harrington–if; Meister–if; Furrier–of; Sagle–if; Maracek–press. (Middle Row L-R): Langendorf–Mgr.; Pryor–of; Radloff–of; Sagle–if; Burlison–P; Williams–of; Thurmer–coach. (Front Row L-R): Wrozier–coach; Wirtz–coach; Jett–c; Wirtz–batboy; Quillman–ss; Miller–c; Smith–p; Welby–general mgr. Courtesy of: Steve Thurmer

The Toronto, New Orleans, and Washington franchises folded before the first pitch. To get the league up to six teams, Chattanooga joined the league's other teams: the St. Louis Browns, Charlotte Panthers, Mobile Gulls, Philadelphia Patriots, and the Montreal Royals.

The St. Louis Browns played their games at Kennedy Stadium in the City of Florissant's Koch Park. Unlike the other cities, the Browns expected and got a good attendance. Their stadium was set to hold 4,000 people and the fans showed up in force to watch the new league. The Browns success came thanks to an awesome offense teamed with steady defense and brilliant pitching. John Redloff, Larry Vowell, Dick Furrier, and Clem Quillman provided the big bats while Roy Burlison crafted an amazing season on the mound. Burlison went 25-2 with an earned-run average of 1.63 while striking out 295 batters in 220 innings.

As the season ended, the Browns, with a record of 39-8, sat atop their nearest opponent, Philadelphia, by 17 ½ games. In the playoffs, they would play the third place team, the Montreal Royals, in the World Series because they were the only team in the league who could afford to come to St. Louis. Philadelphia and Charlotte had been operating in the red since midseason. Montreal's chances of winning were summed up with the simple fact that Burlison had beaten them 10 times in 10 decisions.

The Browns won the World Series by sweeping the Royals in 4 games that were all played at Koch Park. Montreal didn't want to play a home game because their attendance at home was so dismal. With all the financial troubles and teams dropping out, it was no surprise when the league folded after the season. The St. Louis fans' turnout throughout the season had kept the Browns—and to a large extent the league—going. In the end, the Browns could not pay everyone else's bills, and thus the last professional team named the St. Louis Browns went out, ironically, with the title of "champions."

Women's Softball Takes Off

★ ★

In 1976, three years after men's Major League Softball began its sole season of play, former LPGA pro Janie Blaylock, softball legend Joan Joyce, and tennis star Billie Jean King founded the International Women's Professional Softball Association (IWPSA). The league opened with 10 teams ranging from New England to Southern California. A St. Louis team called the Hummers (short for hummingbirds) joined the league the next year along with a team from Bakersfield, California. In 1976, it would only be a six-team league before dropping to four teams the next year and back up to six in 1979. The league's season initially comprised a 120-game schedule consisting of 60 doubleheaders. Players were paid a salary ranging from $1,000 to $5,000 a year as they traveled the country at the teams' expense to play the game they loved. As with so many other professional sports endeavors, the high cost of travel and upkeep led to the league's demise after the 1979 season.

The Hummers were more than a fad and a startup. They were all-in with stars from across the country when they began play in 1977. Pitchers Margie Wright and Cindy Henderson teamed with sluggers Pat Guenzler (who led the league in hitting 3 times), Nancy "Boomer" Nelson (1979 League MVP), and Vicki Schneider to make a potent squad managed initially by St. Louisan Bob Umfleet and then player-manager Linda Wells over the course of the team's three seasons. While the Connecticut team would win the league all four years, the Hummers were formidable during their time. They came in second in 1977 and 1978 and won their division in 1979 only to lose in the World Series. For many of these girls, it was not just an honor to play professional softball; it was a dream come true to play in their hometown before friends and family. The team had a nucleus of local talent in Guenzler (Affton High School), Schneider (McCluer North High and then Meramec Community College), Charlene Sennwald (Ursuline Academy), and Linda Wells (Pacific High School). Wearing orange and brown colors reminiscent of the St. Louis Browns, the Hummers regularly attracted thousands to Hummers Park in the Harrawood Complex located along the Meramec River in Valley Park (a western suburb of St. Louis). Not only did fans come to the park to watch them play, the games were often televised across the St. Louis region on KDNL Channel 30.

The Hummers played during a period when Major League Baseball was going through a contentious labor period (a strike in 1972 and lockouts in 1973 and 1976). In a July 1977 article in the *St. Louis Post-Dispatch*, one fan talked about coming out to see the Hummers. "I'm getting sick of big league baseball. I'd take a Hummers game over the Cards any day." Another fan said, "The Hummers have got more hustle than the Cards . . . Maybe if you paid the Cards less money, they'd work a little harder. I'm coming back here." Not only did the Hummers offer fans a lot of down-home friendliness, one of their supporters from Washington University noted that "the Hummers are quietly tearing down sexual barriers in sports."

For three years, the Hummers would be leaders in league attendance, averaging about 1,800 fans, yet only filling about half the stadium. And as with so many other teams, good or bad, it always comes down to money. Despite the league-leading attendance, the team could not cover its expenses. Like so many other leagues and teams across the sports world over time, without money and the loss of BIC Pen as a sponsor, the league would fold. Yet they left their mark on their fans and especially all the area's young girls, who would dream of one day taking the field like their favorite Hummer.

Basketball

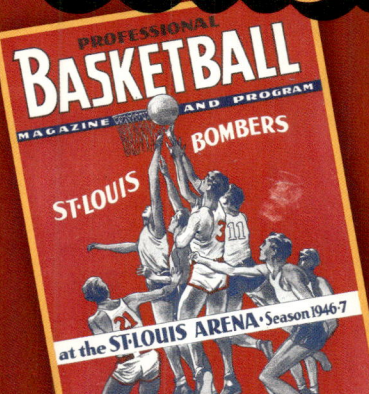

GET THE BASKETBALL SPIRIT

Cliff Hagan
Courtesy of: Wikimedia Commons

Courtesy of: Jim Eschenbrenner

1947: (left to right) Don Martin, Bob Doll, Belus Smalley, John Logan, and George Munroe of the St. Louis Bombers pose for a portrait. Courtesy of: Getty Images

Bob Pettit
Courtesy of: Wikimedia Commons

Spirits of St. Louis basketball player Moses Malone, who would go on to win the NBA's Most Valued Player Award three times. Courtesy of: Wikimedia Commons

Hoops Madness in St. Louis

The St. Louis region's off-and-on history of professional basketball has kept the sport somewhat obscured in the annals of the city's sports history. Yet the city has definitely had some very special runs and players that left their mark on the sport. In local gyms, playgrounds, field houses, and arenas, St. Louis was like all cities where basketball became a game that kids of all ages could play whether as an amateur or a pro. And across the city and region, success was found at all levels.

It's a history that has spanned two teams in the National Basketball Association (NBA) and another in the American Basketball Association (ABA). In the 19 seasons of professional play in St. Louis, just one World Championship was won while teams here produced 12 players and coaches who have been enshrined into the Naismith Memorial Basketball Hall of Fame. There have been magical moments in the sport that mirror David slaying Goliath, as a hometown star helped the city's namesake university defeat the "Big Apple's" team for a college national title. And that same local fella did it again a decade later, leading the city's second professional team to the town's only NBA Championship.

After the Hawks hooped their way to Atlanta after the 1967 season, the professional basketball spirit would wane until 1974, when an ABA team took the court for a two-season run at the St. Louis Arena. Even without a professional-level team, amateur, high school, and college basketball continue to keep the eyes of the sport on the St. Louis region.

Both images courtesy of: Rich Noffke

SLU's Home-Grown Boys Win It All

★ ★ ★ ★ ★ ★ ★ ★ ★ ★ ★ ★ ★ ★ ★ ★ ★ ★ ★ ★

Prior to the mid-1940s, few in the sports world knew anything about Saint Louis University's basketball program. As the 1947 season kicked off, that was about to change. By the following March, that Billikens team would never be forgotten.

First year Coach Eddie Hickey's exciting fast-break game energized both the team and the fans and got the Billikens in the National Invitational Tournament (NIT). The NIT was the premiere national event in college basketball back then, overshadowing the NCAA Tournament as the sport's most prestigious postseason event.

Although the Billikens finished second in the Missouri Valley Conference standings, they were selected for the NIT with just three losses. What was even more amazing was that the dozen Billiken players who became national champions were all home-grown boys. Louis Lehman came from Beaumont High. Bob and Joe Schmidt came from Cleveland High. Joe Ossola was from Collinsville, while team captain D. C. Wilcutt had played at Normandy. Marvin Schatzman was from Soldan, and Clayton Cary, John Cordia, Ed Macauley, Henry Raymonds, and Jack Wrape had all played at St. Louis U. High.

The team headed to New York's fabled Madison Square Garden and rolled over Bowling Green and then Western Kentucky in the

Ed Macauley
Courtesy of: Wikimedia Commons

early rounds. On St. Patrick's Day 1948, the luck of the Irish must have been with the Billikens, who were the underdogs facing New York University in what would be for them a home game. How good were the NYU Violets? They had won 19 straight games heading into the title game. While there was an actual blizzard outside, the 6'8" Ed Macauley was creating a blizzard of his own inside the Garden. While the game had been close in the first half, Macauley took charge in the second. With just 11 minutes, 48 seconds remaining in the game and the Billikens leading 41-24, the string bean of a kid who would soon be known as "Easy Ed" had scored 24 points—the same number as the entire NYU team. The final score was 66-52, but it could have been much more lopsided had Coach Hickey not let his third stringers play the last five minutes of the game.

With the win, Ed Macauley would go home as the tournament's MVP and a St. Louis college team would sit atop the world of college basketball. Three days later, when the team arrived back at St. Louis's Union Station by train, they were greeted by 15,000 fans ready to celebrate with a victory parade. Saint Louis University had gained the respect of the basketball world and would follow with good teams and coaches in the coming decades, but nothing would ever equal that win in 1948. For Ed Macauley, this, however, was just the start.

The Bombers Were First

The St. Louis Hawks, who won an NBA title, were not the first National Basketball Association team in town. That distinction goes to the St. Louis Bombers, who had joined the NBA a decade earlier in 1949 after playing the three previous seasons as one of 11 charter teams in the BAA (Basketball Association of America).

1946-1947 Bombers

Courtesy of: Getty Images

The Bombers home court was the venerable St. Louis Arena. In their first two years, they were coached by future Hall of Famer Ken Loeffler and led by guard Johnny Logan. The Bombers were a decent team but not a great one. They never won a league title, but they did win the Western Division title during the 1947 season only to lose in the semifinals to the Philadelphia Warriors.

The 1949 season began with the BAA and the NBA merging in what would become the Bombers' final season. During their NBA season, the Bombers suited up a player who would become one of St. Louis's greatest basketball assets of all time in future Hall of Famer Ed Macauley. Despite having helped Saint Louis University's basketball team to a national title in 1948, "Easy" Ed's play could not keep the Bombers from finishing last in their division. In the end, their four-year franchise record was barely above .500. They won 122 games while losing 115. At the end of the 1949 season, and after just four years of play, the Bombers closed shop and ceased operations. The players were then dispersed to other teams across the league.

St. Louis bombers Franchise Results

SEASON	LEAGUE	WINS	LOSSES	FINISH
1946-47	BBA	38	23	2nd of 5
1947-48	BBA	29	19	1st of 4
1948-49	BBA	29	31	4th of 6
1949-50	NBA	26	42	5th of 5
	Totals	122	115	0.515

The Hawks Win It All and Leave

★ ★

After the Bombers folded in 1950, it would be five more years before the NBA would return to town. History definitely repeats itself, and just as Milwaukee's baseball club had moved to St. Louis in 1902, the Milwaukee Hawks moved to the Gateway City in 1955 to become the St. Louis Hawks (and like the baseball team, they too would eventually leave). Milwaukee had not been the team's first stop.

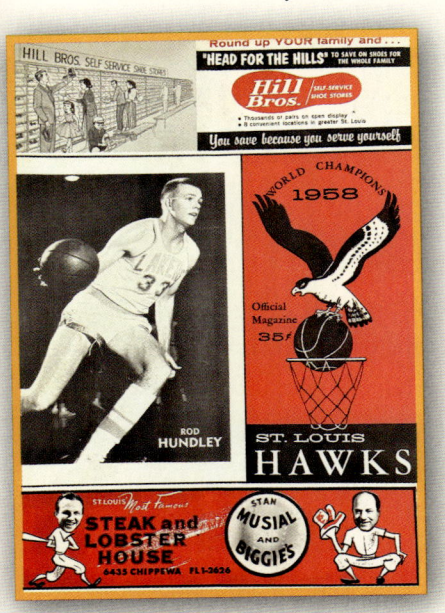

It had originated in Buffalo in 1946 as the Bisons before moving to Moline, Illinois, a year later.

They were called the Tri-Cities Blackhawks due to the proximity of the towns of Moline, Rock Island, and Davenport, and were part of the NBA's original 17 teams in 1949. From there, the team moved to Milwaukee with a shortened name—the Hawks. They were there for four seasons before moving once more to St. Louis. The Milwaukee Hawks were led to St. Louis by coach Red Holzman, a standout player and coach, and future Hall of Famer. The team also brought with it one very special player, the second pick in the first round of the 1954 NBA draft. His name was Bob Pettit, and he will always be remembered as the greatest basketball player to ever play in St. Louis.

The Hawks would spend 13 seasons in St. Louis, playing at Kiel Auditorium (and a few other sites) before moving to Atlanta after the

1967 season. While in the Lou they put up some dominating seasons, starting with a five-year run beginning in 1956 that would result in the first of four appearances in the NBA Finals in the next five years. Alex Hannum had followed Holzman as coach 33 games into the 1956 season after the team had gone 14-19. Holzman would move on to guide the great years of the New York Knicks, but under future Hall of Famer Hannum, the Hawks would make it to the NBA Finals in the 1956 and 1957 seasons. It was in the 1957 season finals that the Hawks won it all, defeating the powerful Boston Celtics 4 games to 2 behind Bob Pettit's 50-point performance in Game 6. That same Celtic team, led by Bill Russell, would defeat the Hawks in their other three trips to the league finals after the 1956, 1959, and 1960 seasons).

Bob Pettit
Courtesy of:
Wikimedia Commons

The Hawks had several stars who contributed to their success. Besides Pettit, players Zelmo Beaty, Chuck Cooper, Richie Guerin, Cliff Hagan, Clyde Lovellette, Slater Martin, Ed Macauley, Rod Thorn, and Lenny Wilkens would run the courts of Kiel all the way to basketball's Hall of Fame. In the end, their record shows the Hawks as a better-than-average team. In the 1,005 games played in St. Louis, they crafted a .550 winning percentage with 553 wins and 452 losses. Besides the single NBA title win, they also won their division five times during their 13-year tenure.

So while there was success on the court, it was a different story at the turnstiles. During their winning seasons in the 1950s, the Hawks would regularly play before 10,000 plus fans at the Kiel, but that was during a time when the baseball Cardinals were the only other professional team in town. By the 1960s, the football Cardinals had relocated from Chicago, and the hockey Blues became the new kids in town in 1967 on their way to three Stanley Cup appearances in their first three years. Professional soccer had also come to the nation's best soccer town when the St. Louis Stars began play in 1967. The Hawks by that time were down to averaging around 5,000 fans per game—even for the playoffs. By the mid-1960s, the team was starting five African American players, and with the civil rights unrest taking place at that time, there are those who speculate that the prominence of these African Americans also kept the crowds away. The Hawks were becoming, in a way, a second-fiddle team and would often get their games moved to Washington University's field house when Kiel was booked. In fact, during their final season, the team played six home games in Miami.

Despite the home-court distractions, the Hawks won the 1967 season's Western Division with a record of 56-26, only to lose to the San Francisco Warriors in the semifinals. It would be the team's final season in St. Louis. The fans weren't showing up and the revenue wasn't coming in, so after the 1967 season, the ownership and the Hawks flew south for new fans and opportunities in Atlanta. Today the Hawks remain a key piece of St. Louis sports history. They reached the NBA finals four times and walked away with a World Championship once. Six other times, they made it to the Division Finals as well as two other trips to the Division Semifinals. Not too shabby a record for their 13-year tenure in the Gateway City, and neither the team's history nor its players should be forgotten.

St. Louis Hawks Franchise Results

SEASON	WINS	LOSSES	W/L%	FINISH	PLAYOFFS
1955-56	33	39	0.458	3rd of 4	Lost W. Div. Finals
1956-57	34	38	0.472	1st of 4	Lost Finals
1957-58	41	31	0.569	1st of 4	Won Finals
1958-59	49	23	0.681	1st of 4	Lost W. Div. Finals
1959-60	46	29	0.613	1st of 4	Lost Finals
1960-61	51	28	0.646	1st of 4	Lost Finals
1961-62	29	51	0.363	4th of 5	None
1962-63	48	32	0.600	2nd of 5	Lost W. Div. Finals
1963-64	46	34	0.575	2nd of 5	Lost W. Div. Finals
1964-65	45	35	0.563	2nd of 5	Lost W. Div. Semis
1965-66	36	44	0.450	3rd of 5	Lost W. Div. Finals
1966-67	39	42	0.481	2nd of 5	Lost W. Div. Finals
1967-68	56	26	0.683	1st of 6	Lost W. Div. Semis
TOTALS	553	452	0.550		

St. Louis's Greatest Basketball Player: Bob Pettit

Professional teams win because they have good players. The St. Louis Hawks were no exception. They had many really good players, including nine who would wind up in the Hall of Fame along with two of their coaches. However, the Hawks had one player who has been recognized as the one of the 50 greatest players in NBA history. His name was Bob Pettit, and he played all 11 years (1954–65) of his storied career with the Hawks (10 in St. Louis and one in Milwaukee). Twice, he was selected as the NBA's MVP (1956 and 1959). His greatness was recognized when he was elected to the Basketball Hall of Fame in 1971.

By the end of his career, Pettit had become the first NBA player to eclipse the 20,000 points mark (20,880 for a 26.4 average per game). His 12,849 rebounds were second most in league history when he retired, and his 16.2 rebounds per game career average remains third after only Wilt Chamberlain and Bill Russell.

Pettit was selected to the NBA All-Star team in each of the 11 seasons he played in the NBA. Four times, he was the game's MVP (1956, 1958, 1959, and 1962). He still holds the top two NBA All-Star Game rebounding performances with 26 in 1958 and 27 in 1962. In addition, he has the second-highest All-Star Game points-per-game average with 20.4, which trails only Oscar Robertson. Pettit was named to the All-NBA First Team 10 times and was named to the Second Team in the other season he played. Simply stated, Bob Pettit is one of the greatest to ever play in the NBA, and we all should remember what he gave St. Louis and its fans.

Pettit in 1958 after being named MVP of the All-Star Game.
Courtesy of: Wikimedia Commons

Was It a Good Trade or Not? Macauley, Russell, and the Ice Capades

★ ★

Interestingly, it was only for less than a day that Bill Russell was a Hawk before becoming a Celtic. What would the franchise have become if he had stayed a Hawk? The future Boston Hall of Famer had actually been drafted by the Hawks in the 1956 draft's first round as the second overall pick. How he got to the Celtics is an interesting story.

After the St. Louis Bombers folded following the 1949 season, St. Louis basketball legend Ed Macauley spent the next six years playing for the Boston Celtics. Macauley blossomed as a leader for the Celts just as he did for St. Louis University. With Boston, Macauley made the All-Star squad all six years (he made one more after the trade to the Hawks). He was actually named the MVP of the very first mid-season classic in 1951 and was named to the first team All-NBA Team in his first three years in Boston as well.

Even with Macauley's stardom, the Celtics had never won an NBA final. They had lost in the Division Finals in six straight seasons. Boston's coach and executive Red Auerbach wanted the big win and wanted the top player in the 1956 NBA draft: Bill Russell. To get him, Auerbach had to do a little manipulation. As Red tells the story, he had to first get the Rochester Royals, who held the draft's first pick, to pass on Russell with the promise that they would receive an Ice Capades performance at their venue. The Celtics team owner was also part owner of the very popular Ice Capades and had promised a lucrative set of dates in Rochester. The Hawks, who held the second pick, weren't quite so easy to bargain with. They demanded and got future Hall of Famer Ed Macauley along with the draft rights of another future Hall of Famer, Cliff Hagan. It was a big-time trade that had big-time results. Russell would help lead the

Celtics to 12 of the next 13 NBA Finals. For 10 straight seasons, from 1956 through 1965, the Celtics won the championship every year except the 1957 season, when they were defeated by the Hawks. The Celtics would also win the title in the 1967 and 1968 seasons. It was sheer dominance led by Russell.

Initially the trade looked pretty fair to both sides, as the Celtics and Hawks would vie for NBA supremacy in the 1957, 1958, 1960, and 1961 season Finals. "Easy Ed" had come back to town and helped deliver the first and only NBA World Championship to his hometown, just like he had delivered the NIT title almost a decade earlier. Still, there were many fans who would wonder what would have happened if the Hawks had held on to Bill Russell. No offense meant towards Macauley or Hagan; both performed well, and both made it to the Hall of Fame, but how dominating would a Hawks team have been if Pettit and Russell had been teammates? Would the pair's dominance have kept the team in St. Louis?

Bill Russell
Courtesy of: Wikimedia Commons

On April 18, 1966, Russell would become the first African American head coach in the NBA when he was named to that position with the Celtics. Ed Macauley completed his stellar 19 year NBA career after the Hawks' 1958 season. He turned in his red and white number 50 uniform for a suit and a seat at the end of the bench coaching the Hawks for the next two years. He took the team to the NBA finals in his last year and, as history would have it, lost to his old team and Hawks nemesis, the Boston Celtics, 4 games to 3. After the season, Ed Macauley left the court and started a long-running career as a television sports announcer in his hometown, St. Louis.

FORGOTTEN TEAMS AND MOMENTS FROM AMERICA'S BEST SPORTS TOWN | 37

The ABA Rolls into Town

★ ★

It was six years after the Hawks left town when the American Basketball Association (ABA) Spirits of St. Louis arrived for a two-year stay. The ABA was an innovative upstart league formed in 1967 as an alternative to the established NBA.

The ABA would stick around for 11 years, bringing excitement and a flashy style of play with new rules and parameters that would eventually be adopted by the NBA. The ABA went with a 30-second shot clock in lieu of the NBA's 24-second clock, and they added the slam dunk contest to their all-star games. More revolutionary was the adoption of the three-point field goal arc. To add more color to the game, the ABA used a red, white, and blue basketball in their games in lieu of the standard orange balls used across the sport.

While fans liked the speed and excitement of the game, the league never had a national television contract and finances were always an issue. Teams would come and go over the 11 years of the ABA. This instability explains how the Spirits got to St. Louis. They had originally been formed in Houston (as the Mavericks) in 1967, before moving to Carolina (and becoming the Cougars) in 1969, and then to St. Louis in 1974.

Named after the plane Charles Lindbergh flew across the Atlantic, the Spirits became a colorful team with some storied players, a famous

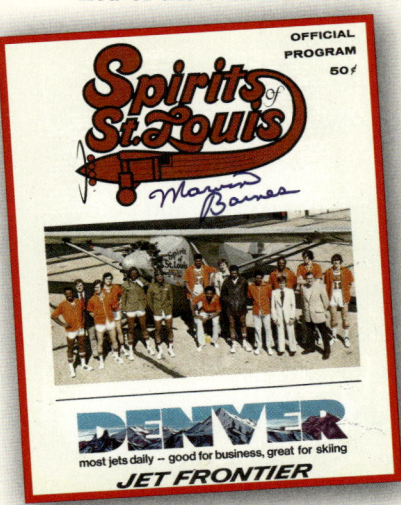

Courtesy of:
Jim Eschenbrenner

announcer, and a Hall of Fame coach. A few of the best players were future Hall of Famer Moses Malone, Maurice Lucas, and Marvin "Bad News" Barnes. The announcer was Bob Costas, who had come to St. Louis at the start of his career on KMOX radio as the radio commentator for the Spirits' games. The coach was Rod Thorn, whose career in the NBA would get him inducted into the Hall of Fame in 2018.

In their two seasons of play, the Spirits never won more than they lost (32-52 and 35-49 in the 1974 and 1975 seasons, respectively). Their franchise winning percentage was a lowly 39.9%. In their first year, they played just well enough to reach the playoffs and upset the reigning ABA champion New York Nets in the first round, 4 games to 1, before losing to the Kentucky Colonels in 5 games in the second round. As in most sports, losing doesn't bring in the fans, and when the team started attracting just over 1,000 fans toward the end of their final year in the 18,000-seat St. Louis Arena, something had to be done.

Ownership had seen enough and started the process that would move the team to Salt Lake City in the coming season. It wasn't just the Spirits having problems. The whole league was in financial trouble, and in the summer of 1976, the ABA worked out a rescue plan with the NBA. There was, however, a hitch in the plan. A merger was proposed between the two leagues, but only four ABA teams would join the NBA. The Spirits weren't one of the four, and so ended professional men's basketball in St. Louis.

The end, however, was not a complete loss for Spirits owners Daniel and Ozzie Silna. One could say it was a slam dunk. As part of their dissolution agreement, the Silnas negotiated a deal to receive 2 percent of NBA television revenues in perpetuity. They would sure make a lot

St. Louis Spirits' Franchise Record

SEASON	LEAGUE	WINS	LOSSES	FINISH	AVG. ATTENDANCE
1974-75	ABA	32	52	0.381	4,618
1975-76	ABA	35	49	0.417	3,728
	TOTALS	67	101	0.399	

more money in that arrangement than trying to get fans in the stands. The Silnas netted over $250 million between the time of the team's demise until a buyout agreement was reached with the NBA in 2014 for an additional $500 million.

There have been a few attempts over the years to revive pro basketball in St. Louis via an NBA expansion team or relocation, but nothing on the scale of the NBA has come to fruition.

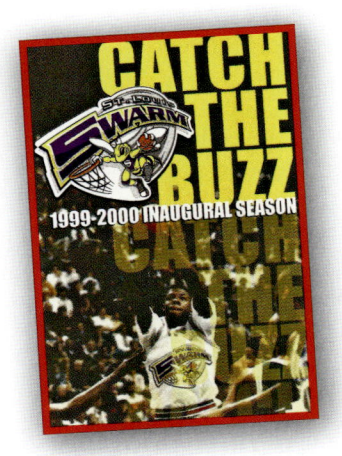

The St. Louis Swarm, part of the International Basketball League's (IBL's) 8-team start-up in 1999, have been the closest thing to professional basketball in St. Louis since the Spirits left. The Swarm played in The Family Arena in nearby St. Charles. They were competitive and won the league's only championships in 2000 and 2001 before the league folded. Since then, St. Louis basketball fans have had to settle for watching the game from afar while cheering on college favorites from the Universities of Illinois and Missouri. For decades, the big basketball event of the year has been the annual "Braggin' Rights" game between these two often-ranked schools.

Near Perfection at the Arena: Bill Walton

Perfection in sports is really not that common. In the 147 years of MLB history, only 23 perfect games have been pitched. The longest streak of consecutive hits is only 11 at bats, held by three MLB players. While bowling the perfect 300 games does happen with a little more regularity, it still is hardly a common achievement. So what would be considered perfection in the sport of basketball?

St. Louis fans and the sports world think it nearly happened at the St. Louis Arena on March 26, 1973. UCLA's Bill Walton put on a shooting demonstration for the ages in that year's NCAA Championship game. For one thing, Walton led his team to their seventh consecutive NCAA Championship; the 87-66 win over Memphis State was their 75th consecutive victory. But those aren't the numbers that had everyone in disbelief.

What made the game memorable was Bill Walton's near-perfect shooting. The junior center scored 44 points during the game. To be sure, there have been collegians who

UCLA's Bill Walton
Courtesy of: Wikimedia Commons

FORGOTTEN TEAMS AND MOMENTS FROM AMERICA'S BEST SPORTS TOWN | 41

have scored more in games. In fact, there have been 26 games since 1955 (per NCAA records) when a player has scored 60 points or more against a Division I school.

So what made Walton's game so special? First of all, it happened in the NCAA finals. This was not against just any school. In this game, the two best teams in the nation were battling it out to be number one. Secondly, it was the near perfection of Walton's shooting. He made 21 of the 22 shots he took. He only missed once, and in that case, he gathered up the rebound and put it through the hoop. That 44 point performance set a record for an NCAA Tournament championship game. Interestingly and despite playing in foul trouble, Walton could have had 52 points—four would-be baskets were waived off for offensive goaltending due to NCAA rules at that time that prohibited dunking.

So over 40 years later, the sports world remains in awe of that March day in St. Louis when Bill Walton displayed near perfection on the St. Louis Arena's basketball court. Today it remains a very special moment in St. Louis sports history.

Wash U's Basketball Dynasty

Across college hoops programs, UCLA is looked upon as the grand-daddy of the sport with its 11 national men's titles since 1939. That run included seven consecutive titles between 1967 and 1973. Kentucky is next with eight; North Carolina has six, while Duke and Indiana have five each.

Washington University in St. Louis celebrates their 65-59 win over Hope College during the Division III Women's Basketball Championship in March 2010 for the national title.
Courtesy of: Getty Images

The Connecticut Huskies women's team has also racked up 11 titles just since 1995. The vaunted Tennessee program is next with eight, and Baylor and Stanford are next on the list with three titles each. So is that the ceiling?

Although it plays at the Division III level, Washington University in St. Louis has claimed seven National Championships in basketball. Under Coach Nancy Fahey, the Lady Bears won five National Titles. They won four straight from the 1997 season through the 2000 season. Fahey's team would win another in the 2009 season, making it five titles in 10 Final Four Appearances. All in all, between the 1986 and 2016 seasons, Fahey would guide the Lady Bears to 29 NCAA tournament appearances. After winning her fifth national title with the Bears, Fahey became the first NCAA Division III coach to be admitted to the Women's Basketball Hall of Fame in 2021. Fahey left Wash U. after the 2016 season with a 737-133 record and a .847 winning percentage before moving to the University of Illinois.

Washington University's men's basketball team had its own national title run when they won back-to-back NCAA Division III titles in 2008 and 2009 under head coach Mark Edwards. That's seven national titles in 13 years for a school known more for scholastics than for athletics.

Volleyball

Fans at the 2016 Division III
Women's Volleyball Championship
Courtesy of: Getty Images

Terri Clemens congratulates her team.
Courtesy of: Getty Images

Kelly Pang (15) of Wash U
Courtesy of: Getty Images

A Volleyball Dynasty Too: Washington University

While Washington University at St. Louis has had an outstanding run in basketball, those accomplishments lie in the shadows of what Coach Teri Clemens's volleyball program achieved at the school. St. Louis became "V. B. Title Town" as Wash U. went on to win 10 NCAA Division III National Championships in 21 years. Clemens won seven of them, including six in a row between 1991 and 1996.

Clemens came to Washington University from Incarnate Word Academy, a suburban St. Louis high school that had a record of 155-15 while winning three consecutive Missouri State High School championships between 1982 and 1984. She would coach the Lady Bears of Washington University for 14 seasons and retire with a .873 career winning percentage—the best in the nation at that time. Clemens' 1992 team's 40-0 record stands as the only undefeated season in NCAA volleyball history.

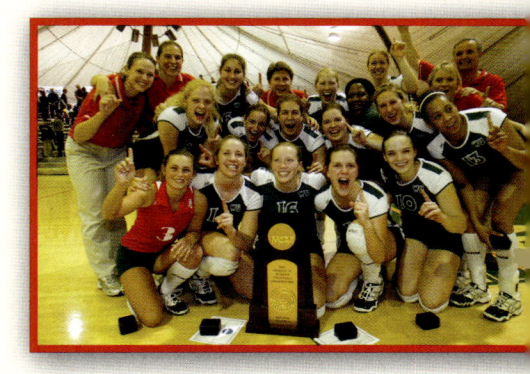

Washington University celebrates their victory over New York University during the Division III Women's Volleyball Championship 30-26, 32-30, 30-22 for the national title in 2003.
Courtesy of: Getty Images

Washington University girls' volleyball continued their success, winning national titles in 2003, 2007, and 2009 under Coach Rich Luenemann. Since the NCAA Division III volleyball tournament began, Washington University sits atop all schools with their 10 championships, followed by the University of California at San Diego with seven wins. Again Wash U. has shown that academic excellence need not come at the expense of athletic success.

Bowling

1958 Record-Setting Series

Don Carter
Courtesy of: Mike Bluth

The Pins Go Down in Bowling Town

After coming to America with the first Dutch settlers, bowling blossomed into the greatest participatory sport in the US between the 1940s and the 1960s. An Anheuser Busch memo sent in the 1950s to their wholesalers supporting the Budweiser Championship Bowling Team noted that, "There are over 20,000,000 bowlers who regularly compete on 60,000 bowling lanes in the USA." Thanks to the brewery and its team of bowlers, there was no better bowling town than St. Louis. The town's history includes some of the greatest bowlers to ever roll the ball as well as some of the greatest performances ever seen. It's a history of records broken and records held.

Bowling can be played by professionals and amateurs on teams or with a group of friends who simply love the sport. In past decades there were almost as many bowling alleys in St. Louis as there were churches. Bowling lanes were first found in saloons where people came to socialize and drink. During the years of Prohibition, bowling alleys began popping

FORGOTTEN TEAMS AND MOMENTS FROM AMERICA'S BEST SPORTS TOWN | 47

Saratoga Lanes, an "upstair-zer" in Maplewood.

up away from the saloons and became more family oriented.

One particular effort brought the city into the sport's spotlight. The first recorded formalized bowling for women began in St. Louis in 1907 thanks to St. Louisan Dennis Sweeney. He was a bowling proprietor, a sportswriter, and one of the first to champion the cause of women in bowling. He helped found the Women's International Bowling Congress in 1916 and received permission to hold a national women's tournament on the American Bowling Congress (ABC) Tournament lanes.

Bowling took off for men and women alike, and bowling alleys began popping up all over town. Still surviving today, Saratoga Lanes in Maplewood is the oldest bowling alley of its type west of the Mississippi and is listed on the National Register of Historic Places.

Almost every business, organization, or church had a bowling team during bowling's glory years. Bowling became a television staple in the 1950s, and as with so many other sports, the bowling eyes of the nation were soon focused on St. Louis. During the late 1950s and 1960s, the city was declared the "bowling capital of the world" and for decades was home to the International Bowling Museum and Hall of Fame.

The Budweisers: Kings of the Lanes

In 1958, St. Louisans Ray Bluth, Don Carter, Tom Hennessey, Pat Patterson, and Dick Weber bowled together on the Budweiser Bowling Team of St. Louis. All were good bowlers, and all would soon wind up in bowling Halls of Fame.

Their places in bowling history were forever etched on March 12th of that year, when they did something that had never been done and would not be done again for almost 36 years. That night, they bowled the highest series in bowling history at Floriss Lanes, located at 4339 Warne in north St. Louis. Together, they shattered—by 61 pins—a bowling record that had stood for 21 years. The irony of the accomplishment is that the previous record was set in 1937 by the Hermann Undertakers, another St. Louis team, who had set their record against a different Budweiser crew.

Front (L to R): Chuck O'Donnell, Pat Patterson, Don Carter, Back (L to R): Bill Lillard, Ray Bluth, Dick Weber, Tom Hennessey. Courtesy of: Mike Bluth

Their record-shattering score of 3,858 pins in their three-game series consisted of 138 strikes in the 150 frames. Putting it another way, their score averaged out to more than 771 pins per man or 257 pins per game for the series. Bluth led the way for team Budweiser, rolling 33 of a possible 36 strikes. The three he didn't make were two spares and an eight. Bluth also rolled a 300 in the third game, matching Hennessey, who put together 18 consecutive strikes while rolling a 300 in the second game. In the end, their individual totals scores were: Bluth 834, Hennessey 759, Weber 775, and Carter 754; an incredible run that for decades kept the spotlight on St. Louis bowling.

St. Louis's Hall of Fame Quintet

★ ★ ★ ★ ★ ★ ★ ★ ★ ★ ★ ★ ★ ★ ★ ★ ★ ★

St. Louis's "Bowling Buds" were the five men who set the bowling record by rolling an ABC-record 3,858 series in Masters League play in March 1958.

Ray Bluth
Courtesy of:
Mike Bluth

⭐ **Ray Bluth** was at the center of the birth of professional bowling and an instrumental leader in getting Anheuser-Busch to sponsor the St. Louis Budweisers. He was the leading bowler in the record-setting series of March 1958. Bluth's "Buds" won five national bowling team match game championships, and he also partnered with Dick Weber to win four National Doubles Championships. He is a member of the PBA (Professional Bowlers Association) and ABC Halls of Fame. His numerous championships include two PBA national titles and an ABC Masters title in 1959.

⭐ **Don Carter** became known as "Mr. Bowling" while dominating the sport during the game's golden age of television. He was a leading force in the formation of the PBA and was elected to its Hall of Fame. He was also subsequently inducted into the ABC Hall of Fame.

Carter had a unique style as he faced the pins. With stooped shoulders and cocked elbows, he made a deep knee bend as he released the ball toward the pins. How big were bowling and Don Carter? In 1964, this 6-time bowler of the year (1953, 1954, 1957, 1958, 1960, and 1962) did something no other athlete in baseball, basketball, football, or golf had ever done. He signed a $1 million marketing endorsement contract with bowling ball manufacturer Ebonite. In 1970 Don was selected in a *Bowling Magazine* poll as the greatest bowler in the sport's history. Three decades later his greatness was again recognized as he ranked second to Earl Anthony in the magazine's poll of the 20 greatest bowlers of the 20th century.

⭐ **Tom Hennessey** was initially a member of the Ziern Antiques bowling team of St. Louis with Ray Bluth, Pat Patterson, and Don Carter before he left town to bowl in Detroit. He came back to St. Louis and joined his former teammates on the St. Louis Budweisers. Hennessey would go on to win four consecutive USBC Open Championship titles between 1962 and 1965 and would be inducted into the USBC Hall of Fame in 1976.

Tom Hennessey
Courtesy of: Getty Images

⭐ **Pat Patterson** may have been the low-scoring man when the St. Louis Budweisers set the record, but his was a career that paralleled his early teammates Ray Bluth, Don Carter, and Tom Hennessey. He was an original member and eventual captain of the Budweiser team. He and his team would win six Bowling Proprietors' Association of America (BPAA) team championships and the USBC Open Championships in 1962. He would be inducted into the USBC Hall of Fame in 1974.

Pat Patterson
Courtesy of:
Mike Bluth

Welcoming Dick Weber to Team Budweiser
Courtesy of: Mike Bluth

⭐ **Dick Weber** is one of the most accomplished bowlers in the history of the sport, winning every bowling award possible. He won 26 national tour titles and six senior championships, including the BPAA US Open four times. He is a member of the ABC and PBA Halls of Fame. Named Bowler of the Year in 1961, 1963, and 1965, Weber became the first bowler to record PBA titles in six consecutive decades when he won a PBA title in 2002. His son Pete followed his father's exploits with his own Hall of Fame bowling career.

Still None Better: Team Budweiser

★ ★

When Team Budweiser set the 3,858 pins record in a three-game series in 1958, they broke a record of 3,797 pins that had been set by another St. Louis team, the Hermann Undertakers, at the Del-Mar alleys on January 27, 1937. The Hermanns had a combined total of 3,797 pins from Sam Garofalo (759), Ray Holmes (792), Fred Taff (766), Bob Wills (771), and Buzz Wilson (709). The Hermanns became the first team in bowling history to pass the 1,300 pin mark in a single game with a score of 1,325.

Team Budweiser's 3,858 pins record stood for almost 38 years until the Hurst Bowling Supplies team of Luzerne, Pennsylvania, bested the score by 10 points. In the ensuing decades, the records have come and gone.

Interestingly enough, in looking at the current USBC records, the St. Louis region continues to rank at the top of them all and the record once owned by the Budweisers is once again held by a St. Louis team.

On March 10, 2016, a team with the moniker The BJ's brought the five-player team, three-game series record back to St. Louis. They bowled their record-breaker at the now shuttered Show-Me Lanes. With a record 3,986 pins (which has not been surpassed since), they bested the record by 49 pins when they took the record away from the Pro Bowl West team from Chattanooga, Tennessee. Pro Bowl West set their mark in March 2009. Within their record-setting performance, the team fell just two strikes shy of tying the 142-strike record for total strikes in a team series.

The record-setting BJ's (L to R): Jay Bradshaw, Linda Bradshaw, John Bogacki Jr., Jana Luden, and Jim Luden. Courtesy of: Jana Luden

The BJ's (a branding based on their first and last names) consisted of Jay Bradshaw (826), Jana Luden (805), Jim Luden (801), John Bogacki (794), and Linda Bradshaw (760). During their record-breaking run, Bogacki was the only one of the five to

Team: The BJ'S	1st	2nd	3rd	Totals
Jay Bradshaw	289	278	259	826
Jana Luden	279	237	289	805
Jim Luden	267	268	266	801
Linda Bradshaw	269	234	257	760
John Bogacki, Jr.	215	300	279	794
Games 1 to 3 Pins	1319	1317	1350	3986
+HDCP	0	0	0	0
Totals	✓1319	✓1317	✓1350	✓3986

Courtesy of: Jana Luden

bowl a 300 game in the series. So while St. Louisans today hold the five-player three-game series record, another group from the region also holds the highest five-player team's score for a single game.

The St. Louis Shelter Insurance team set the current five-player world record of 1,457 pins in a single game on February 28, 2020. The team that night was playing the Fairway Mortgage team in the Tri-Challenge Friday Night League at Concord Bowl. The Shelter team was comprised of Greg Getzlow, Tom Grimm, Mark Hood, Tom Shucart, and Ron Testa. In that first game of the series they knocked down 55 strikes in 58 opportunities and broke a standing record at that time of 1,434 pins (still 3rd-highest all-time) that had been rolled in 2011 by a team from Lindenwood University in the St. Louis suburb of St. Charles. The Shelter team wasn't a bunch of college boys either. The five members were all over 50 years old. Grimm at 53 was the youngest, and everyone else was over 60. It was in their opening game of the series that their record-breaking night began with a string of 27 strikes. The streak ended when Grim left a 10 pin in the sixth frame. In all, there would be 55 strikes in 58 opportunities.

The record setting Shelter Insurance team (L to R) Mark Hood, Ron Testa, Greg Getzlow, Tom Grimm, and Tom Schucart. Courtesy of: Ron Testa

Courtesy of: Ron Testa

Getzlow tossed a tenth strike before a 9 pin ended his bid for a 300 game. Ron Testa and Tom Schucart, however, did get the perfecto. While just 43 pins away from total perfection in their game, their 3,789 series was still 197 pins shy of the BJ's series record. And with their special games, these two teams and 10 bowlers still sit atop the leader boards and have left their mark with two remarkable moments in bowling and St. Louis history.

Known as the Buckets on Deck, the Lindenwood team (comprised of Connor Druhm, Eddie Cetwinski, E. J. Parks, Brad Miller, and Ryan Council) set their aforementioned 1,434 record at Harvest Lanes in St. Peters. Ironically, they broke the standing record at that time of 1,413 pins (still fifth-highest all-time) set by St. Charles's O. T. Hill's team, which consisted of Jim Hankemeyer, Mike Goodin, Randy Lightfoot, Leroy Bornhop, and John Weber (Hall of Famer Dick Weber's son).

The long history of St. Louis bowling greatness continues today with St. Louisans still sitting atop the various record books of the sport.

A Hall of Fame Comes, and a Hall of Fame Goes

★ ★

During its golden years of the 1950s and '60s, St. Louis was bowling's epicenter. So it was appropriate that the International Bowling Museum and Hall of Fame be located there when it opened in 1984 as a showcase of the sport whose history St. Louis had dominated.

The Museum and Hall of Fame were located across the street from Busch Stadium within a triangle-shaped building that also housed the St. Louis Baseball Cardinals Hall of Fame. Perhaps in the end, that contributed to its demise. It seemed like a great draw—two Halls of Fame for the price of one—and just like the baseball side of the building, the bowling exhibits and memorabilia provided a great history of the game and the people who ruled the sport. A paid admission would also allow visitors to bowl a game on vintage lanes from past eras.

In time, the building's land was needed for the construction of the new Busch Stadium in 2006. The Cardinals offered to relocate the Bowling Hall of Fame to a new building just up the street in the soon-to-be-constructed Ballpark Village, but the brain trust of bowling instead sought their own independent positioning so as not to be overshadowed by the aura of baseball.

In October 2008, the facility and its collections moved to the International Bowling Campus in Arlington, Texas, housed alongside the USBC, which is the governing body for amateur bowlers as well as the BPAA.

FORGOTTEN TEAMS AND MOMENTS FROM AMERICA'S BEST SPORTS TOWN | **55**

Strikes and Spares and Memories Galore

★ ★

Bowling alleys flourished across the region as the sport became increasingly popular during the middle of the 20th century. It was not uncommon to see a bowling alley inside a bar or even a church basement. Standalone alleys began popping up everywhere and carried the names of their communities or nearby landmarks. Others had names that reflected their ownership, like Ray Bluth, Don Carter, Dick Weber, or even baseball greats like Terry Moore, or Redbird Lanes, jointly owned by Joe Garagiola and Stan Musial.

There were bowling alleys known as "upstair-zers," like Saratoga Lanes, where the lanes were on the second floor of the building. The Floris Lanes actually had bowling on two floors. There were eight lanes on the building's second floor and another eight on the third floor.

Each alley was unique and had its own special history. One of the most storied alleys of all time was the Arena Bowl, sitting on the western side of the St. Louis Arena parking lot on Oakland Avenue. When it opened in May 1957, it was heralded as one of the largest bowling centers in the country, with 48 lanes. For the next three decades it became a bowling institution and became even more famous after surviving a tornado's direct hit in February 1959.

Originally used as a livestock exhibition hall, the building was owned by the Wirtz family of Chicago (owners of the NHL Chicago Blackhawks). In addition to the bowling lanes, the building also housed a roller rink that was eliminated in the post–1959 tornado remodeling that added an additional 24 lanes in order to keep up with the bowling boom of the late 1950s.

One of the most memorable events that took place at the Arena Bowl occurred between 1976 and 1980. An afternoon television program called *Bowling for Dollars* was filmed at the Arena Bowl by television station KTVI and hosted by Morgan Hatch. The premise was that contestants could bowl to win cash and sometimes prizes based upon their bowling skills. Station KDNL had aired *Bowling for Dollars* from 1973 to 1976, but it was filmed in house in their studios with Russ Davis as host.

Over the next two decades, faced with steep maintenance costs as well as a decline in bowling's popularity, ownership found they could make more money tearing the building down and adding parking space for events at the adjacent Arena. The end came when the lanes closed in October 1985, and the wrecking balls soon turned the facility, home to decades of memories, into just another parking lot. Now, with the bowling alley and the Arena itself both gone, few St. Louisans today recognize while driving along Highway 40 / 64 the importance of that Oakland Avenue site just east of Hampton Avenue.

Not too far as the crow flies from St. Louis sits a collegiate bowling powerhouse. The McKendree College team won their second NCAA women's bowling national championship in six years in 2022. The Bearcats had won the title in 2017 and had come in second in the nation in 2018.

First home game program

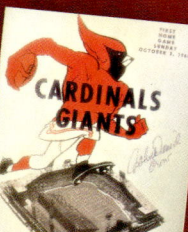

St. Louis All-Stars

Football

1981 ST. LOUIS FOOTBALL CARDINALS

Owner Bill Bidwell
Courtesy of:
Getty Images

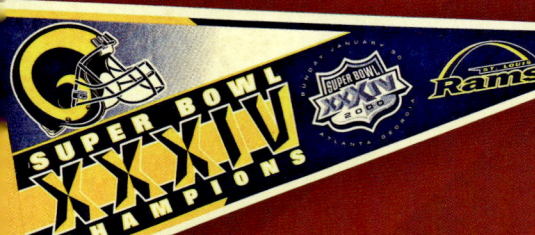

Courtesy of:
Bill and Richard Hudson

The Forward Pass

★ ★ ★ ★ ★ ★ ★ ★ ★ ★ ★ ★ ★ ★ ★

Football came to the Midwest and St. Louis like so many things throughout our nation's history, arriving on the East Coast from Europe and then spreading westward over time. Football's roots are within the game of rugby, which was brought across the Atlantic by immigrating Europeans. The sport has undergone many changes since the first documented game was played between college rivals Princeton and Rutgers on November 6, 1869. Today football has eclipsed baseball as America's top sport, and it was a St. Louis team from over a century ago that is credited with creating one of the most popular components of today's game: the forward pass.

Quarterback Bardbury Robinson Courtesy of: Wikimedia Commons

Rule changes to the game in 1906 made the forward pass legal. Long before its prominence as a soccer powerhouse, Saint Louis University (SLU) had a football team. While other schools were also trying to reinvent the game under the new rules, most credit SLU's coach Eddie Cochems with guiding his team's Bradbury Robinson to throw the first legal forward pass on September 5, 1906. His first attempt, however, fell incomplete and became a turnover due to the rules of those days. Later in the game Robinson completed a 20-yard touchdown pass to Jack Schneider to lead SLU to a victory over Carroll College and an 11-0 season. With their creation and use of the forward pass, SLU became the most potent offense in college football and went on to outscore their opponents that year 407-11. It was a prequel to a future St. Louis team's "greatest show on turf." Decades later, Hall of Fame coach and football authority David Nelson wrote that "Eddie Cochems is to forward passing what the Wright brothers are to aviation and Thomas Edison is to the electric light." It totally changed the game of football, and it all started with a team from St. Louis.

NFL 1-2-3-4

★ ★

There have been four MLB teams in St. Louis and, surprisingly, four teams from the National Football League (NFL) have called St. Louis home as well. Initially known as the American Professional Football Association (APFA), the league began its inaugural season in 1920 with 10 teams in four states. Two years later, it renamed itself as the NFL. St. Louis was not one of those inaugural teams, but in 1923, the St. Louis All-Stars were invited in for a short one-year run. Eleven years later, the Gunners would appear for an even shorter three-game stay in the league, and then for almost three decades, St. Louisans would only be reading about NFL football from afar.

Courtesy of: Steve Thurmer

As the 1960s rolled around, the NFL began challenging the MLB for the top spot of sports entertainment. St. Louisans' thirst for football was soon quenched when the Bidwill family moved a mediocre Cardinals team from Chicago to St. Louis. Good or bad, it was football, and it was back in the Gateway City. While there were seasons of nail-biting excitement and last-minute comebacks, the Cardinals' general play was unexceptional, which then led to something of a love–hate relationship between the team, its fans, and city officials that eventually led team ownership to relocate the team to Arizona after 28 seasons.

A period of eight years without NFL football in St. Louis ended when a former St. Louis showgirl brought her inherited team—the Los Angeles Rams—back to her hometown for what would be called the "Greatest Show on Turf." The Rams brought St. Louis something the town had never seen before—a playoff win. But soon afterward the showgirl died, and another battle began that left St. Louis without an NFL team once more.

Not Many Stars on the All-Stars

As with so many other franchises in the world of sports, the NFL All-Stars' tenure in St. Louis was short and disappointing. Coach Ollie Kraehe definitely did not field an explosive team. In their first-ever game they visited the Green Bay Packers on October 7, 1923, and came away with a 0-0 tie. The next week, they played their first home game before 2,831 fans at Sportsman's Park against the Hammond Pros from Hammond, Indiana, and once again finished in a 0-0 tie.

It would be another month before they would score their only points and win their first and only game when they defeated the Oorang Indians from LaRue, Ohio, 14-7. Interestingly, that game featured the only scoring the team would have in its entire season, and both scores were made by Potosi-born Pete Casey. One was on a touchdown pass from quarterback Eber Simpson and the other was on a fumble recovery that Casey ran back for a touchdown. The All-Stars finished 14th in the 20 team league, and the plain and simple truth was that the team was not very good. It folded after a single season in the NFL.

St. Louis All-Stars One Year NFL Record

Score

DATE	OUTCOME	RECORD	OPPONENT	ALL-STARS	OPPONENTS
October 7	Tie	0-0-1	Green Bay Packers	0	0
October 14	Tie	0-0-2	Hammond Pros	0	0
October 21	Loss	0-1-2	Cleveland Indians	0	6
October 28	Loss	0-2-2	Milwaukee Badgers	0	6
November 4	Loss	0-3-2	Green Bay Packers	0	3
November 11	Win	1-3-2	Oorang Indians	14	7
November 24	Loss	1-4-2	Milwaukee Badgers	0	17

The Replacement Gunners

★ ★ ★ ★ ★ ★ ★ ★ ★ ★ ★ ★ ★ ★ ★ ★ ★

It would be another decade before NFL football would return to the Gateway City, and that team had an even shorter stay than the All-Stars—just three games. The St. Louis Gunners became an NFL replacement team in 1934 when the NFL's second-year Cincinnati Reds couldn't complete the last three games of the season. By 1934, the NFL had been pared down to just 10 teams, and the Reds were by far the worst, having lost their first eight games while being outscored 243-10. When the Reds could no longer pay their league dues and were expelled during the 1934 season, the St. Louis Gunners were brought into the NFL to complete the season schedule. While not affiliated with a given league, the Gunners had been successfully playing as an independent professional team across the country. The Gunners had gotten their start back in 1931 as a team from the 128th Field Artillery of the Missouri National Guard. They were headquartered out of the Guard's Armory, which was the source of the name "Gunners." Future NFL Hall of Famer and St. Louisan Jimmy Conzelman was the team's first coach. Over the next three seasons the team would play their games at St. Louis Public School Stadium, Sportsman's Park, and Washington University's Francis Field. In three years of independent play, the team had an impressive 23-8-5 record and had beaten multiple NFL teams in exhibition games.

In August 1934, the Gunners sought to buy the lowly Cincinnati Reds NFL franchise but were turned down by the NFL due to St. Louis's distance from the league's other teams. The other teams did not want the additional travel expense—something that would impact other St. Louis sports franchises in the future. The Gunners also

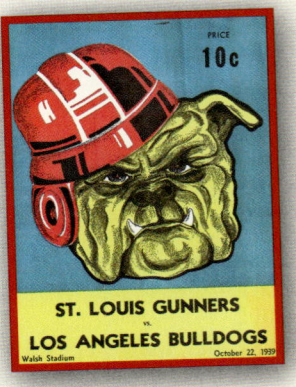

Courtesy of: Steve Thurmer

rejected a bid to join the minor-league American Football League (AFL) that year. The AFL would eventually form and host a team called the St. Louis Blues in 1934. In the meantime, the Gunners continued playing independent football and had started the 1934 season 5-0 when the NFL suspended the 0-8 Reds for failing to pay their league dues. On November 6, 1934, the NFL approved the sale of the Reds to the Gunners for approximately $20,000, and they immediately began playing the next weekend at Sportsman's Park. To avoid a split fan base, the AFL's St. Louis Blues moved to Kansas City.

The Gunners under coach Chile Walsh won their first game against the Pittsburgh Pirates 6-0 at Sportsman's Park on November 11. The next week, they got trounced in a 40-7 loss to the Detroit Lions. They then finished the season at home with their third and final game against the Green Bay Packers—a 21-14 loss and a combined (including Reds games) last place finish. Probably the only bright spot of their NFL tenure was that they scored more points (27) in their three games than their city predecessors, the All-Stars (14), had in a full season 11 years earlier.

The NFL dropped the Gunners from their 1935 season and played with one fewer team in the Western Division until 1937, when they added the Cleveland Rams, a team that would eventually be a part of St. Louis's NFL history. Without a spot in the NFL in 1935, the Gunners joined the AFL and played in that league until it too folded after the 1939 season. They then went back to playing an independent schedule beginning in 1940.

St. Louis Gunners 1934 Season

DATE	OUTCOME	RECORD	OPPONENT	GUNNERS	OPPONENTS	LOCATION
November 11	Win	1-0	Pittsburgh Pirates	6	0	Sportsman's Park
November 18	Loss	1-1	Detroit Lions	7	40	U. of Detroit Stadium
December 2	Loss	1-2	Green Bay Packers	14	21	Sportsman's Park

The Third Time's a Charm (Sort of): The Cardinals

★ ★ ★ ★ ★ ★ ★ ★ ★ ★ ★ ★ ★ ★ ★ ★ ★

After the Gunners left the NFL, St. Louis would be without the big-league football team for almost 25 years. The next team to arrive would stay a little longer than the first two had. The Cardinals franchise was one of the NFL's original charter teams. In fact, the Cardinals are the oldest professional football team in terms of continuous operation. They date back to their founding as the Morgan Athletic Club in 1898. When the Cardinals eventually decided to leave the shadow of their Chicago neighbors, the Bears, they came to St. Louis and would stay for 28 seasons before leaving for Arizona in 1988 after the city rejected their requests for improvements.

The Chicago Cardinals' ties to St. Louis began long before their 1960 relocation. In Chicago, the Cardinals had had some success, having won NFL Championships in 1925 and 1947. The Cardinals' 1947 team had the famed "Million Dollar Backfield" of Paul Christman, Charley Trippi, Elmer Angsman, and Pat Harder. Their two championship wins were two more than the team would get in the Gateway City.

The Chicago Cardinals were owned by Charles Bidwill Sr., and upon his death in 1947, the team's ownership went to his widow, Violet. Charles died before his team won the title, not only making Violet the first female principal owner of an NFL team but also making the Cardinals the first female-owned team to win the championship. Ironically, the St. Louis Cardinals baseball team had the first female principal owner in their league, and then 35 years later, another female owner of an NFL team would move her team from Los Angeles to the Gateway City and win an NFL title.

The Cardinals experienced a quick fall from the top heading into the 1950s and wound up with a single winning season during the entire decade. Violet Bidwell eventually remarried a businessman from St. Louis named Walter Wolfner, and the St. Louis connection was established. In the meantime, the Cardinals were falling from grace with Chicago fans, whose allegiance to the crosstown Bears was growing stronger as a result of the Bears' success. When the fans and revenue weren't supporting the Cardinals, the Bidwills (Violet and her sons Bill and Charles Jr.) sought to relocate their team. However, the NFL had a very hefty relocation fee that the Bidwills could not afford. While several groups were interested in purchasing the team, the Bidwills wanted to maintain control. It was also during this period that the American Football League (AFL) was back, gaining strength, and looking to expand. For the Bidwills, things soon fell in place. The NFL, realizing the dire situation in Chicago, also wanted to block the AFL from moving to St. Louis, so they agreed to the move of the Cardinals to St. Louis to start the 1960 season.

The first lady NFL owner Violet Bidwill (right), Walter Wolfner (left), and head coach Joe Kuharich (center) at Lake Forest, Illinois, training camp in 1952.

On Friday, September 23, 1960, under the direction of coach Pop Ivy, the St. Louis Cardinals football team traveled to California for their first game, which just happened to be against another relocated team. The Cardinals came away with an impressive 43-21 win over the Los Angeles Rams, who had relocated from Cleveland at the start of the 1946 NFL season. Was this win and the move to St. Louis the start of great things to come?

FORGOTTEN TEAMS AND MOMENTS FROM AMERICA'S BEST SPORTS TOWN | **65**

The team would lose their next three games before squeezing out a win over the Dallas Cowboys on their home field at Busch Stadium (the renamed Sportsman's Park). To avoid confusion with the baseball team of the same name that they shared the city and stadium with, St. Louis's football team was often lovingly referred to as "the Big Red." They won the next two games of their inaugural season before trading wins and losses the rest of the way. Behind quarterback John Roach and the likes of John David Crowe, Joe Childress, Bobby Joe Conrad, and Sonny Randle, the Big Red finished fourth out of six teams in their division with a record of 6-5-1. Would a new city and an above-.500 record be a precursor of things to come?

In the ensuing 28 seasons, the Cardinals called St. Louis home, there were many good players and exciting teams. During the mid- to late 1970s, the team became known as the "Cardiac Cards" because they often found a way to come from behind late in games. In the 1975 season alone, eight of their games were decided in the final minute of play, and the Cardinals came out ahead in seven of them.

Four St. Louis Cardinal players—Dan Dierdorf, Jackie Smith, Roger Wehrli, and Larry Wilson—would wind up enshrined in the Football Hall of Fame. Over the years, the team was led by quarterbacks Charlie Johnson and Jim Hart pairing with running backs including Johnny Roland, McArthur Lane, the Anderson boys (Donny and Otis), Jim Otis, Terry Metcalf, and Stump Mitchell. There were many outstanding receivers to throw to when Bobby Joe Conrad, Sonny Randle, Jackie Smith, Mel Gray, Roy Green, and Pat Tilley took the field. The Cardinals' offensive line was so good that in 1975 they set an NFL record by allowing only eight quarterback sacks. Those guardians of the backfield were Roger Finnie, Bob Young, Tom Banks, Conrad Dobler, and the NFL's best offensive lineman of the decade, Dan Dierdorf.

The defensive side of the ball had some great players as well, starting with Larry Wilson and Roger Wehrli, as well as Pat Fischer, Dale Meinert, and Curtis Greer. And no one can forget the sure footed, straight-on kicks of Jim Bakken, who saved many a game with his last-minute field goals.

Despite the excitement and some regular-season success, the team never had a playoff win. The Cardinals only had 10 winning seasons in their 28 years and only made the playoffs three times (1974, 1975, and 1982). When they did, they never played a playoff game at home, and each time they were in the playoffs, they bowed out rather quietly.

Violet Bidwill Wolfner died in 1962 and left the team to be run by her two sons, Bill and Charles Jr., also known as "Stormy." Bill would eventually buy out Stormy in 1972. The franchise's one bright spot happened in 1964. It wasn't a championship win, but a consolation win. The two second-place teams of each division would meet in the Playoff Bowl, originally called the Runner-Up Bowl, for third place in the NFL. In that year's event, the second-place Football Cardinals met and defeated the Green Bay Packers 24-17 in the "third-place bowl" played in Miami's Orange Bowl. The lackluster play of the team in the ensuing years, along with questionable draft picks, eventually led to a fans-versus-owner tug of war. The fans felt the owners weren't doing enough to win and wanted a winner. The owners wanted a stadium comparable to what other teams were playing in to enhance revenues.

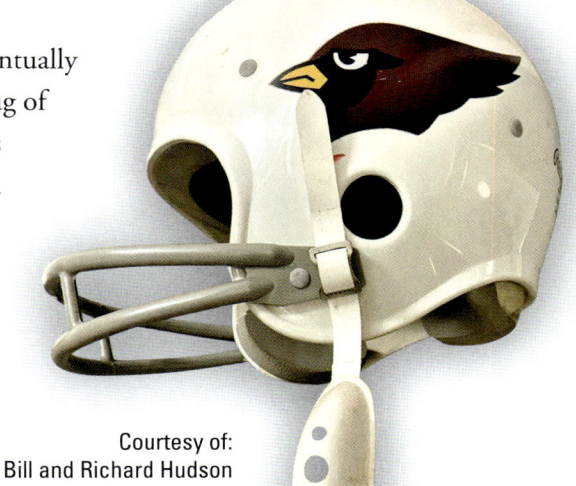

Courtesy of:
Bill and Richard Hudson

1987 ST. LOUIS FOOTBALL CARDINALS

KMOX Radio 1120   America's Sports Voice

Politicians soon got in the middle of the tussle, which led to no stadium and moving trucks headed to Arizona. The St. Louis Football Cardinals' last game was a 27-24 win over the New York Giants on December 13, 1987. They left with a winning percentage of .463, which happens to be higher than those recorded by the franchise in either Chicago or Arizona.

An interesting side note in Cardinal football history had happened two decades earlier when Bidwill wanted a better stadium than Busch Stadium I (the renamed Sportsman's Park), where fans had to walk out on the field to access a portable grandstand. He threated to move to Atlanta in 1964 but was appeased with the 1966 opening of Busch Stadium II. Shortly after Bidwill's play for Atlanta, the St. Louis Hawks took his lead, moving their franchise there in 1967.

St. Louis Cardinals Franchise Results

SEASON	WINS	LOSSES	TIES	WIN %	DIVISION PLACE	POINTS FOR	POINTS AGAINST
1960	6	5	1	0.500	4th of 6	288	230
1961	7	7	0	0.500	4th of 7	279	267
1962	4	9	1	0.286	6th of 7	287	361
1963	9	5	0	0.643	3rd of 7	341	283
1964	9	3	2	0.643	2nd of 7	357	331
1965	5	9	0	0.357	5th of 7	296	309
1966	8	5	1	0.571	4th of 8	264	265
1967	6	7	1	0.429	3rd of 4	333	356
1968	9	4	1	0.643	2nd of 4	325	289
1969	4	9	1	0.286	3rd of 4	314	389
1970	8	5	1	0.571	3rd of 5	325	228
1971	4	9	1	0.286	4th of 5	231	279
1972	4	9	1	0.286	4th of 5	193	303
1973	4	9	1	0.286	4th of 5	286	365
1974	10	4	0	0.714	1st of 5	285	218
1975	11	3	0	0.786	1st of 5	356	276
1976	10	4	0	0.714	3rd of 5	309	267
1977	7	7	0	0.500	3rd of 5	272	287
1978	6	10	0	0.375	4th of 5	248	296
1979	5	11	0	0.313	5th of 5	307	358
1980	5	11	0	0.313	4th of 5	299	350
1981	7	9	0	0.438	5th of 5	315	408
1982	5	4	0	0.556	3rd of 5	135	170
1983	8	7	1	0.500	3rd of 5	374	428
1984	9	7	0	0.563	3rd of 5	423	345
1985	5	11	0	0.313	5th of 5	278	414
1986	4	11	1	0.250	5th of 5	218	351
1987	7	8	0	0.467	3rd of 5	362	368
	186	202	14	0.463		8300	8791

Georgia Brings Them, and Stan Takes Them

★ ★ ★ ★ ★ ★ ★ ★ ★ ★ ★ ★ ★ ★ ★ ★ ★ ★ ★

The most recent NFL franchise to call St. Louis home—the Rams—got to the Gateway City via Cleveland by way of Los Angeles. The team began in Cleveland in 1937 and moved to the West Coast in 1946. On July 13, 1972, Robert Irsay bought the Rams from the estate of the late Dan Reeves. Carroll Rosenbloom had owned the Baltimore Colts since their re-entry into the NFL in 1953. After issues erupted over Baltimore's stadium in 1972, Rosenbloom essentially did an owner's swap, trading his Colts for Robert Irsay's Rams.

Johnny Unitas (left) and Owner Carroll Rosenbloom (right)
Courtesy of: Getty Images

Rosenbloom had success with the Johnny Unitas–led Colts, and he quickly continued a tradition of winning with the Rams. In fact, Rosenbloom had the best winning percentage of any owner in NFL history with 226 wins, 116 losses and 8 ties to go along with 3 NFL championships (1958, 1959, and 1968) and a win in Super Bowl V. So the Rams had an owner and were a franchise unlike anything previously seen in St. Louis. But Rosenbloom never intended to move to St. Louis. The team's relocation came about after he died suddenly in 1979 and left the team to his wife, a former St. Louisan named Georgia Frontiere.

Rams owner Georgia Frontiere
Courtesy of: Getty Images

70 | ST. LOUIS SPORTS MEMORIES

Rosenbloom's winning ways were not passed on to Frontiere in the inheritance. The Rams were losing in Los Angeles while sharing the city with the Raiders, who had moved south from Oakland. The Raiders were winning, as were other Los Angeles sports teams at the time. As the Rams fans were fleeing and revenues were falling, Frontiere first proposed a move to Baltimore. The Baltimore Colts had moved to Indianapolis in 1984, but Baltimore would not have a team again until the Ravens arrived in 1996. Frontiere's proposed move to Maryland having been turned down by the NFL, she then sought to relocate to her hometown of St. Louis. While initially turned down once more, her threat of legal action caused the league to rethink its opposition. St. Louis committed to building the Rams a taxpayer-financed stadium that, per the agreement, was to be maintained and upgraded so that it would remain in the top 25% of all NFL stadiums. Everyone in St. Louis rejoiced that they were once again back in the NFL and paid little attention to that key clause of the relocation agreement.

History once more repeated itself. The Rams were now the second team in NFL history to be led by a female, and like Violet Bidwill, Georgia Frontiere had skirmished with the NFL big boys about relocating to St. Louis. In the end, each got their way. Ironically neither of their teams would stay.

The Rams came to St. Louis under Coach Rich Brooks in 1995 ready to play football but initially without a stadium or a practice facility. They would play their first games in the Cardinals' Busch Stadium II while their new domed stadium was being finished. Their practice field would be at a local high school—

First Game in St. Louis Ticket

Parkway Central Senior High School in Chesterfield. Their inaugural season got off to a good start with a 17-14 win in Green Bay, and they then treated their new hometown fans to a 17-13 homecoming win over the New Orleans Saints on September 10.

They got another win the next week against Carolina and another the following week against the Bears. Football had a different vibe than had been experienced with the city's previous teams—or so it seemed. However, the team's fortunes soon changed. After playing and winning their first game in their new domed stadium on November 12, they stood at 6-4. They would win only one more time and finish with a 7-9 season record. It was starting to look like the same old, same old again . . . but having even a mediocre NFL football team was better than not having one at all, as St. Louisans knew all too well.

The Rams would stumble through three more losing seasons before something never seen before in St. Louis would happen. Playoff football would actually come to St. Louis for its fans to see in person. After going 15-33 between the 1996 and 1998 seasons, the 1999 Rams took off. They went 13-3 under third-year coach Dick Vermeil and made it to the playoffs.

After 35 combined seasons of NFL football in St. Louis, there had never been a playoff game played in the Gateway City, and now, during the 1999 season, there would be two. And during those 35 combined seasons there had never been a meaningful playoff game played by a St. Louis team. The Cardinals playoff teams had played on the road and had lost each of their three playoff games by a combined score of 106-53. In the 1999 postseason, the Rams would win three times by a combined score of 83-59.

Behind MVP Kurt Warner, the Rams would defeat the Minnesota Vikings 49-37 and the Tampa Bay Buccaneers 11-6 at home before defeating the Tennessee Titans 23-16 on January 30, 2000, in Super Bowl XXXIV, held in Atlanta's Georgia Dome. Looking back, there are those that might say the Championship was "won by a foot" due to

Mike Jones's game-saving tackle of the Titans' Kevin Dyson inside the one yard line as the clock ran out.

The turnaround that got the Rams to the Super Bowl sounds like something from a Hollywood film script. The reality of the 1999 team's accomplishments became just that with the 2021 release of the film *American Underdog*. The stars of the season and the film were a quarterback who a year earlier had been stocking shelves in a grocery store in Iowa, an NFL head coach who had been out of the game for 15 years, and an offensive coordinator dubbed "Mad Mike" due to his style of play calling. It became an offense like no other previously seen in the NFL. The puzzle pieces named Warner, Vermeil, Martz, Faulk, Bruce, and Holt fit perfectly together to be dubbed "The Greatest Show on Turf." As a team, they racked up the points and wins that would send the Rams back to the Super Bowl two years later. Unfortunately, they experienced the rise of the Bill Belichick and Tom Brady dynasty. After their second Super Bowl in three years, the Rams went from the top and owning their division to its bottom looking up. Front office issues, poor coaching, and eventually Georgia Frontiere's death revealed the "death star" mentality of the team's new owner, Stan Kroenke. The Rams would play their last home game on December 17, 2015. Two road games would follow, and then it was over,

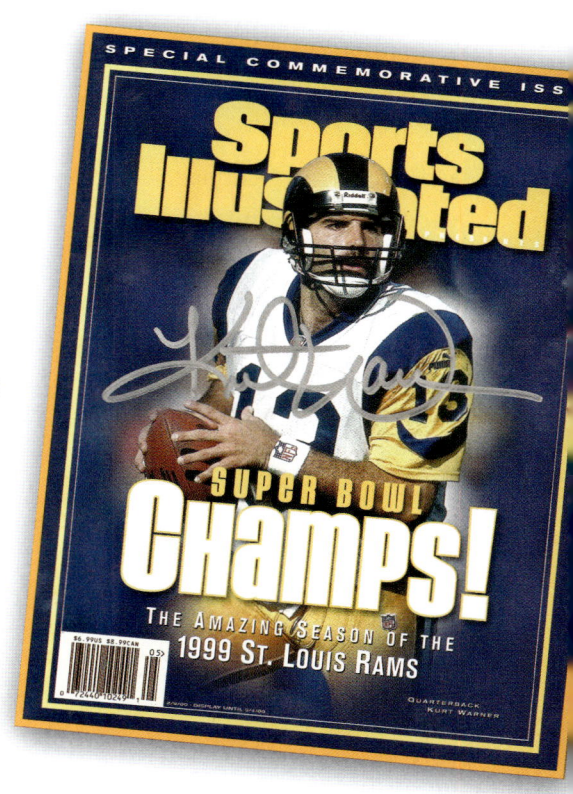

St. Louis Rams owner Georgia Frontiere holds the Lombardi Trophy as quarterback Kurt Warner (L) and head coach Dick Vermeil (2nd R) look on after Super Bowl XXXIV. Courtesy of: Getty Images

Kroenke took his team to Los Angeles.

A November 2021, $790-million legal settlement between Kroenke, the NFL, and the city of St. Louis laid out Kroenke's behind-the-scenes efforts to move the Rams to Los Angeles while playing a shell game with the city of St. Louis and its fans. Even with the settlement, the Rams were gone, and once again Georgia's hometown was without an NFL team. The settlement's payout to the city was meant to compensate for financial damages, but it could not erase the disdain for the city shown by Kroenke and the league, nor could it give St. Louis fans the Sunday joy of watching their hometown football team.

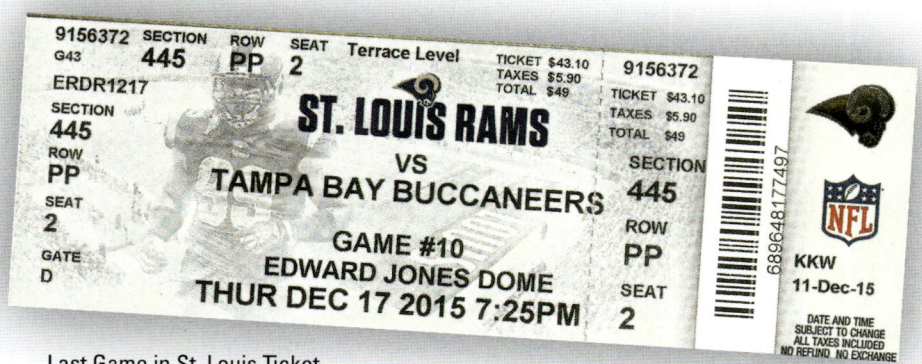

Last Game in St. Louis Ticket

74 | ST. LOUIS SPORTS MEMORIES

St. Louis Rams Results

YEAR	WINS	LOSSES	TIES	WIN %	DIV. FINISH	PLAYOFFS	COACHES
1995	7	9	0	0.438	3rd of 5		Brooks
1996	6	10	0	0.375	3rd of 5		Brooks
1997	5	11	0	0.313	5th of 5		Vermeil
1998	4	12	0	0.250	5th of 5		Vermeil
1999	13	3	0	0.813	1st of 5	Won SB	Vermeil
2000	10	6	0	0.625	2nd of 5	Lost WC	Martz
2001	14	2	0	0.875	1st of 5	Lost SB	Martz
2002	7	9	0	0.438	2nd of 4		Martz
2003	12	4	0	0.750	1st of 4	Lost Div	Martz
2004	8	8	0	0.500	2nd of 4	Lost Div	Martz
2005	6	10	0	0.375	2nd of 4		Vitt, Martz
2006	8	8	0	0.500	2nd of 4		Linehan
2007	3	13	0	0.188	4th of 4		Linehan
2008	2	14	0	0.125	4th of 4		Haslett, Linehan
2009	1	15	0	0.063	4th of 4		Spagnuolo
2010	7	9	0	0.438	2nd of 4		Spagnuolo
2011	2	14	0	0.125	4th of 4		Spagnuolo
2012	7	8	1	0.438	3rd of 4		Fisher
2013	7	9	0	0.438	4th of 4		Fisher
2014	6	10	0	0.375	4th of 4		Fisher
2015	7	9	0	0.438	3rd of 4		Fisher
TOTAL	142	193	1	0.423			

Ka-Kaw and More: The XFL

✯ ✯

It wasn't NFL football being played in St. Louis's Dome at America's Center, but it was still football. After four seasons without big-time football, the XFL began play in the Gateway City. St. Louis football fans were looking for something—anything—to rally around. There weren't any NCAA Division I teams in the metro area to cheer on. There had been several attempts at different levels of professional football; many had tried and died playing in various arena football leagues. But the XFL had a different appeal.

The XFL was originally a league that began, and folded, in 2001. It was formed by Vince McMahon, a man known more for professional wrestling than football. With his financially successful WWE portfolio, it looked like there was hope for this new endeavor.

While most people assumed the "X" in XFL meant extreme, McMahon said it stood for "anything but the NFL, which he considered stuffy and boring." St. Louis fans were ready to jump on board with anyone who was anti-NFL and brought big-time football to town. McMahon promised simplified rules to make for a faster-paced game played by former college and NFL players.

The St. Louis BattleHawks were one of eight inaugural teams in the revived XFL that began play in 2020.

Logo decal and hat Courtesy of: Bill Hudson

ST. LOUIS SPORTS MEMORIES

Courtesy of: Getty Images

The BattleHawks would lead the league in fan attendance and television viewership during their short tenure. The team scored on their first drive of their first game against the New York Guardians on February 23, 2020, before 29,554 fans in the Dome. There was hope for good, fun football, but four weeks later, the shadow of the COVID pandemic ceased the league's operations and ended the BattleHawks' season with a 3-2 record. The league filed for bankruptcy, and wrestling legend Dwayne "the Rock" Johnson soon became the league's new owner. It has since been announced that play would begin on February 18, 2023, with St. Louis being one of the eight host cities. That same announcement named former NFL tight end Anthony Becht as the St. Louis franchise coach. During the course of his 11 year NFL career, Becht spent the 2008 season in St. Louis with the Rams. Although still to be determined whether the team will keep the BattleHawk moniker, the one thing that is certain is professional football will once again be played in the Dome!

An Arena Alternative: The AFL

You can play soccer in an arena, so why not football? The Arena Football League (AFL) became very popular across the country after its 1987 debut. It was played in many non-NFL towns and provided an offseason (May to September) football fix for fans. In 1995, the St. Louis Stampede joined the AFL's 13 other teams.

The Stampede's run would only last for two years even though the AFL would last until 2019. As they say, "timing is everything." The Stampede kicked off their first game just months before the Rams would move to St. Louis. The team was initially welcomed, with an average attendance of over 10,000 fans for their 6 home games. The team responded with a 9-3 season but was upset in their first playoff game by the Albany Firebirds.

The next year, the Stampede slipped to third place in their division with an 8-6 record and again lost in the first round of the playoffs, this time to the eventual AFL champs—the Iowa Barnstormers, led by future Ram hero Kurt Warner. Whether it was the emergence of the Rams or the team not winning in the postseason, average attendance dropped 35 percent in 1996 and the team subsequently folded.

What followed was a long history of arena football leagues and teams coming and going in St. Louis. Most played at the Family Arena in St. Charles. The Renegades began play in 2001 in the Indoor Professional Football League and went 2-11. The league folded at year end. In 2002, the RiverCity Renegades joined the National

Courtesy of: Steve Thurmer

Indoor Football League but posted a 1-13 record. The team took a new name for the next two seasons, the Show-Me Believers. They went 4-10 and 9-5 respectively. A winning edge gave them another new name and they became the River City Rage. The team would play under that nickname from 2005 to 2009, going 46-26 with some success but no championships. Despite improvement, the end came after the 2009 season due to financial struggles.

Even though history shows sustaining a league or a team is difficult, they seemed to keep popping up every year or two. Between 2013 and 2017, the Family Arena entertained teams in the Ultimate Indoor Football League, X-League Indoor Football, American Indoor Football, and Arena Pro Football with franchises named the Missouri Monsters, St. Louis Attack, and River City Raiders.

These attempts at establishing football teams were not limited to the men's efforts. Women's football even came to town in different forms and levels of attire. The St. Louis Saints was a proposed entry into the Lingerie Football League (LFL) in 2013 that would play at the Family Arena. It was a league where the women took the field in sports bras, shorts, shoulder pads, and a helmet. Even though the LFL would operate in one form or another between 2009 and 2019, it never made its debut in St. Louis. Despite holding tryouts and lining up a team, the operators of the Family Arena in St. Charles could not get the necessary financial guarantees from the league and felt that a team "wasn't a good fit and didn't make sense from a business or public relations standpoint."

Courtesy of: Rich Noffke

In contrast to the LFL, the St. Louis Slam played in the National Women's Football Association (2003–2008) and then the Women's Football Alliance beginning in 2009. It was a true 11-on-11 tackle football league played outdoors at Lindenwood University. The Slam even had a measure of success. They have been active in all but four seasons since the league's inception and have gone 106-35, winning 4 championships (2006, 07, 17, and 19). Whether the league can return after the COVID pandemic is yet to be seen.

All of these teams and leagues played football in one form or another and drew some level of fan interest. Some had financial support, and others didn't—and soon folded. St. Louis football history has had turmoil driven by the league, its owners, and often the politicians. The one thing that remained constant was the fans. In the end, all these teams took the field, played their games, and were part of the St. Louis region's football experience and memories.

Hockey

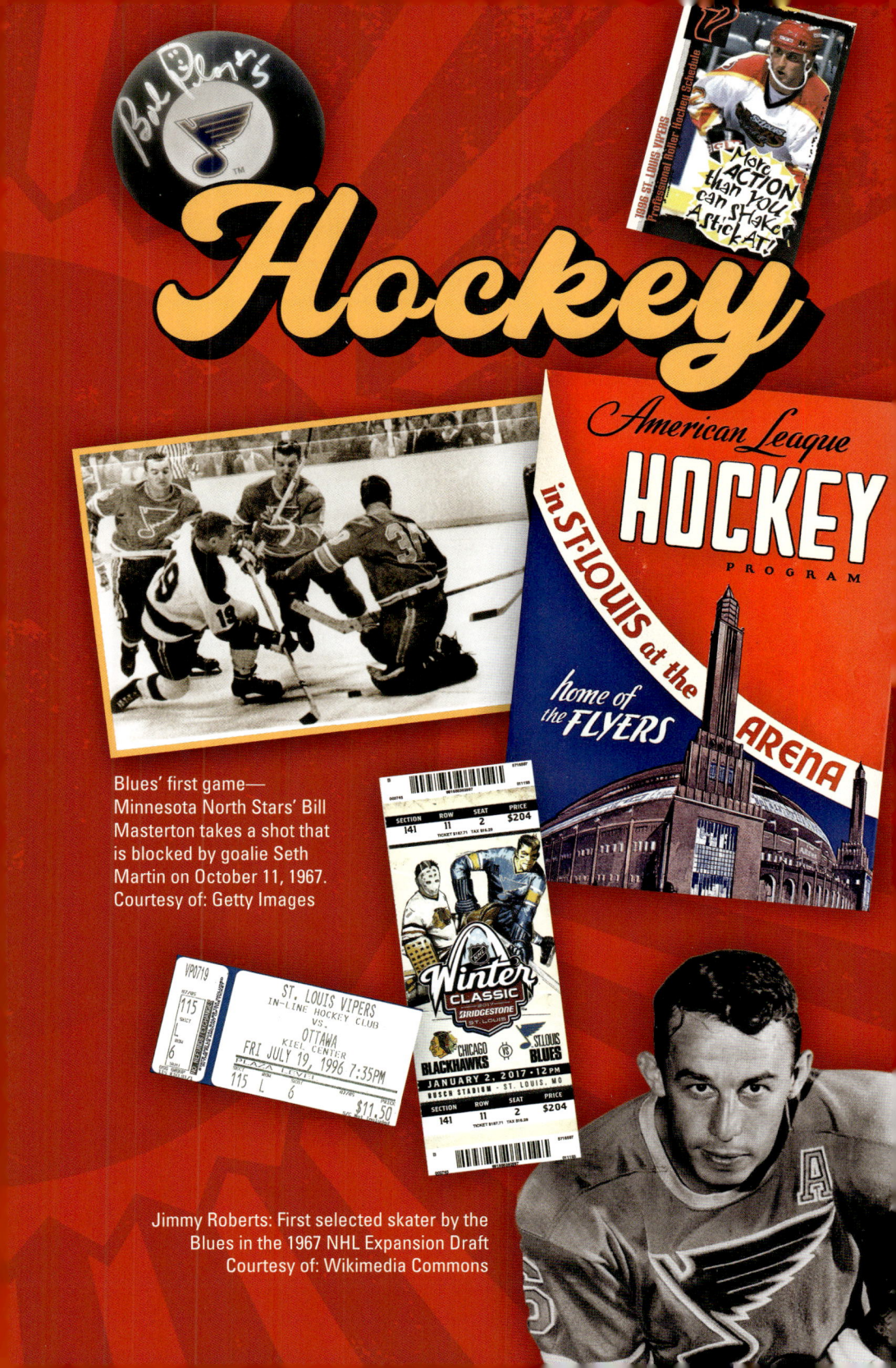

Blues' first game—Minnesota North Stars' Bill Masterton takes a shot that is blocked by goalie Seth Martin on October 11, 1967.
Courtesy of: Getty Images

Jimmy Roberts: First selected skater by the Blues in the 1967 NHL Expansion Draft
Courtesy of: Wikimedia Commons

The Puck Dropped Long before the Blues: The Flyers

★ ★ ★ ★ ★ ★ ★ ★ ★ ★ ★ ★ ★ ★ ★

When the Blues came "marching in" to St. Louis during the 1967–68 season, the city immediately rallied behind the team, and the Blues reciprocated with three straight appearances in the Stanley Cup Finals. However, these new kids on the block, or should we say "ice," were not the town's first hockey experience. In fact, they weren't even the city's first National Hockey League (NHL) team. The sport had existed for decades on both the amateur and professional levels.

Courtesy of: Jim Eschenbrenner

The minor-league Flyers led the way, playing 14 seasons in the American Hockey Association (AHA) from 1928 to 1942. The team began playing their games at the Winter Garden Ice Rink built during the 1904 World's Fair. The rink was located at DeBaliviere and Kingsbury Avenues, just north of Forest Park. In time, they moved to the St. Louis Arena. After a year off for WWII, the Flyers played another nine seasons at the Arena as part of the American Hockey League (AHL) between the 1944 and 1952 seasons.

The AHA Flyers had some success during their 14 seasons, making it to the league finals six times with wins in the 1934, '35, '37, '38, and '40 seasons. They lost in the finals in 1933 and '36. The AHL version wasn't as accomplished. In their nine seasons they only made the playoffs twice (1948 and 1949 seasons) and lost both times in the first round.

St. Louis Flyers Results

		GAMES	WINS	LOSSES	TIES
1928-1942	Flyers AHA	666	352	263	51
1944-1953	Flyers AHL	599	235	297	67
	TOTAL	1265	587	560	118

The Eagles Fly In

A few years after the Flyers began play, the St. Louis Eagles (inspired by Anheuser-Busch's logo) became the city's first NHL team, but only for the 1934–35 season. The St. Louis Arena would be their home ice. It would also be the NHL's only stadium with segregated seating. Prior to relocating, the team had been playing as the Ottawa Senators since 1883. They moved to St. Louis, then the nation's seventh-largest city, due to financial issues. Ottawa was the NHL's smallest market.

The move didn't bring the financial boost needed to keep the team in St. Louis. Not only were they competing with the successful Flyers at the same venue, but the NHL made things worse by keeping the Eagles in the Canadian Division, meaning they were playing the teams located farthest from St. Louis. The travel expenses added to the financial challenges that soon had the owners looking to move once more.

Ironically, the NHL had rejected a St. Louis bid for a team in 1932 because the expected travel cost to and from the Lou was deemed too expensive in the pre-airline days of the Great Depression. They should have remembered that decision before approving the Eagles' move two years later. After their lone St. Louis season, which ended with a record of 11–31-6 and a last place finish, the league bought the franchise, ceased its operations, and dispersed the players to other teams. In 1938, the NHL would deny the Montreal Maroons' attempt to relocate to St. Louis due to the high travel costs faced by the Eagles. It would be another three decades before the NHL would drop the puck once more in the Gateway City.

St. Louis Eagles
Courtesy of: Jim Eschenbrenner

One More before the Blues: The Braves

★ ★ ★ ★ ★ ★ ★ ★ ★ ★ ★ ★ ★ ★ ★ ★ ★ ★ ★ ★

Before the Blues brought the NHL back to town, there would be one more professional hockey team playing in St. Louis. It wasn't an NHL team, but rather the St. Louis Braves, a minor league affiliate of the Chicago Blackhawks. The Braves arrived in town in mid-season from Syracuse, New York, in January 1963. The move from Syracuse made sense; the Braves' owners were the NHL's Chicago Blackhawks co-owners Arthur Wirtz and James Norris, and they just happened to also own the St. Louis Arena. The Braves would play in St. Louis through March 1967, at which time they moved to Dallas to make room for the city's NHL return.

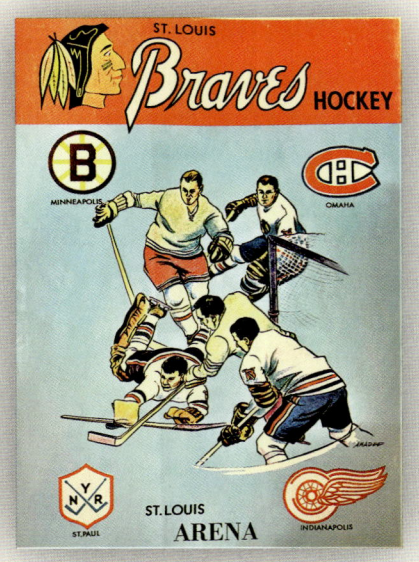

The Braves came to town coached by future Blues announcer Gus Kyle. They were an up-and-down team. In the 1963 season, they would lead the league in scoring with 316 goals while giving up only 275. Alain Caron was their goals (77) and scoring (125) leader. Future Blues nemesis and future Hall-of-Famer Phil Esposito was a powerhouse with the Braves in that first year, scoring 80 points in just 43 games before being called up to the Blackhawks. Other Blackhawk notables who spent time in the Lou were Wayne Maki, Lou Angotti, Fred Stanfield, and Pat Stapleton.

The next season, the Braves were the worst goal-scoring team in the league. They scored only 187 goals while giving up a league-worst 329 goals. In the two seasons, they made the playoffs (1963 and 1965) they were bounced out in the first round. In the end, their record shows that they just were not a very good team.

When the NHL began talks to expand the league beyond its original six cities, Norris and Wirtz proposed including St. Louis on the list. The city's central geographic position fit the NHL's footprint of westward expansion. With a capacity of over 17,000, the St. Louis Arena would become the second-largest venue in the NHL behind only the Blackhawks' Chicago Stadium. The hitch in the plan was the NHL's guidelines forbidding owners from maintaining an interest in more than one club and preventing a team from being a tenant of another club. Therefore, Wirtz and Norris would need a buyer for their Arena as well as someone wanting a hockey team to play there.

And that is where the Blues came into the picture. Insurance tycoon Sid Solomon Jr. was just the man they were looking for. He put together a group, which included Cardinal great Stan Musial, that would win the expansion bid and purchase the Arena, leading to the Braves moving to Dallas, where they played for the next 15 seasons as the Blackhawks.

St. Louis Braves Results

	WINS	LOSSES	TIES	WIN %
1963-64	33	32	7	0.458
1964-65	13	51	6	0.186
1965-66	30	31	9	0.429
1966-67	24	26	20	0.343
TOTAL	100	140	42	0.355

The Blues Come Marching In

★ ★

Sid Solomon and the Blues certainly did come marching in in 1967 and immediately won the hearts of the town's sports fans. Being new and successful is fun. It also puts the fans in the stands. It must also be remembered that the town's big sports team, the St. Louis Cardinals, was also winning and would win the World Series in 1967 and another pennant the following season. But the symbiotic relationship of the two winners and the fans worked well; the Blues caught on and have now lasted well over a half-century. Even though they made it to the Stanley Cup Finals in their first three seasons it wouldn't be until their 51st season that the Blues would once again make it to the Finals and finally get to drink from Lord Stanley's Cup.

The Blues joined the California Seals, Los Angeles Kings, Minnesota North Stars, Philadelphia Flyers, and Pittsburgh Penguins as part of the NHL's 1967 six-team expansion. The expansion teams were all placed in the Western Division, while the Eastern Division contained the original six NHL teams. Ironically, during the expansion talks, history was about to repeat itself once more. St. Louis was not the league's first choice for the new team—Baltimore was initially the favorite. But unlike a decade earlier, when the Browns went to Baltimore, the Blues came to St. Louis at the urging of the Blackhawks ownership.

Besides owning the Blackhawks, James Norris and Arthur Wirtz owned the Arena, which was in need of significant maintenance and repairs. There are also those who have said the "Chicago boys" wanted to establish a team of "loveable losers" modeled after their "Windy City" baseball team. Looking back, the winds of change provided just the right climate for Solomon's group to put millions into the renovation and seating expansion of the Arena, and with the smart leadership of general manager Lynn Patrick, they found just the right mix of players within the expansion draft.

The Blues 27-31-16 record in the inaugural season under Coach Scotty Bowman earned them 3rd place in the division when the playoffs rolled around. Bowman had taken over for Patrick, who had initially served both as general manager and head coach, but had stepped down from the latter after a poor 4-13-2 start in 1967. To get to the finals, the Blues had to overcome Philadelphia and then Minnesota each time in seven games, before facing and being swept by the Montreal Canadians in the Stanley Cup Finals. The first season was a definite success and set the tone for decades to come.

Coach and general manager Lynn Patrick (left) and the team owner Sid Salomon III model home and away uniforms.
Courtesy of: Getty Images

As with the baseball Cardinals, the Blues' history and players have been well documented and well known. Ever since the first puck dropped in a Blues regular season hockey game on October 11, 1967 (a 2-2 tie against Minnesota), there have been many moments of magic and heroics. There have been four Stanley Cup Finals appearances and finally, after half-a-century, a win. There have been 28 Hall of Famers who wore the "blue-note" sweater and many more fan favorites who skated the length of the ice or guarded the crease between the pipes. Memorable names like "Barc the Spark," the Red Baron, the Iron Man, the Golden

Brett, the Great One, Petro, and Binner are just a few from a franchise roster that is filled with great players. Was it Hull and Oates (a play on the name of a pop duo of the time) or "Shanny" and Oates who repeatedly put the "biscuit in the basket," as long time radio commentator Gus Kyle used to say in the early days of the Blues?

There have also been those memorable moments across Blues history that began with Larry Keenan's opening night goal and Noel's trip of Orr. There were goalies without masks, Red's six, and a fight in Philly with Blues in the stands. Then came the Monday Night Miracle, the St. Patrick's Day Massacre, the Winter Classic, and finally "Gloria." With the good, there was also the bad and disruptive, and at times there seemed to be too much of the latter that prevented the team from skating all the way to the Cup. The team's history is one of coaching changes and ownership turnovers that yielded periods of success and periods of setback. Has there ever been another professional team that went through its sport's annual players draft without making a single pick? It happened with the Blues in 1983. A frustrated Ralston Purina ownership was so upset over the NHL's denying the sale of the team to Saskatoon that they refused to let team personnel participate in the draft and thus cost the franchise future depth and talent. However, Ralston's biggest fingerprint on the franchise occurred when they painted the Arena with their brand's checkerboard squares and renamed it "The Checkerdome."

88 | ST. LOUIS SPORTS MEMORIES

Although they have hoisted the Stanley Cup only once, the Blues have played good hockey over the years and rewarded their fans by consistently getting to the playoffs. They have been to the postseason 45 times in their 54 years in the league (83% of the time) which is more than any other team outside the "original six." Since hockey's expansion in the 1967–68 season, the Blues have the second-most playoff appearances of all NHL teams and have made 4 trips to Lord Stanley's Cup Finals. They just haven't gone as deep as they could have. But the fans still come, and through it all, there was always the soothing voices of a broadcast team led by Hall of Famer Dan Kelly that kept it all in perspective. They would keep the fans believing and coming back while listening as the Blues "skated left to right on your radio dial." And unlike other teams that have come and gone, the Blue's fans kept coming throughout the years. Finally, they were rewarded with the elusive Stanley Cup following the 2019–2020 season.

The St. Louis Blues celebrate their Stanley Cup victory on June 12, 2019.
Courtesy of: Getty Images

SLU Takes the Ice

When people think of Saint Louis University (SLU) sports, their first reaction is usually either basketball or soccer. But back in 1970, when St. Louis was abuzz about hockey and the Blues, the Billikens suited up and took to the ice in a Division I college hockey program. The team played their games in the largest home venue in the college ranks—the Arena.

St. Louisans and college and high school students filled the seats to be a part of the city's hockey craze while watching an exciting, less-expensive alternative to the Billiken's NHL landlords. And how the fans enjoyed it. On February 17, 1974, the hockey Bills set a record for college hockey's largest crowd when 15,346 fans showed up to watch the Billikens wallop the Ohio State Buckeyes 8-3 in a nonconference game. That evening's attendance broke the previous record of 14,995 set at the Boston Garden in March 1972 when Boston University beat Cornell in the NCAA Tournament's Championship game. Hockey had taken St. Louis by storm at all levels.

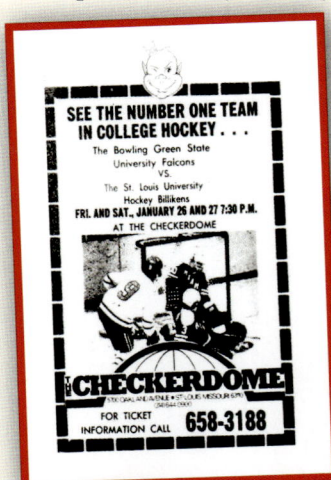

In a show of determination to be a major player in the sport, the university hired a proven leader, Bill Selman, as head coach. Selman had taken the North Dakota Fighting Sioux to back-to-back appearances in the NCAA Hockey Tournament in prior years.

During their inaugural season, the Billikens had no conference affiliation and played as an independent. That year could be called an evolving year, as they finished with a 9-19-2 record. The next year, they helped form the Central Collegiate Hockey Association (CCHA) and began taking big strides by finishing second in the league with a 15-15-3 record and taking second place in the conference tournament. During the next six years they were either first or second in the standings or in the tournament. In their final season, when the fate of the program was written on the wall, they slid to fifth place.

Even though there was some instability and changing college teams within the CCHA, the real blow to the SLU program came from their landlord—the St. Louis Blues. In 1977, Sid Solomon's ownership group sold the Blues and the Arena to Ralston Purina—a national feed and cereal conglomerate headquartered in St. Louis. Sid Solomon and his team were people pleasers, but the new owners were businessmen and were out to make money on their investment. They forced a new, more expensive lease arrangement on the university during a time when SLU was working through its own budget issues. The increased costs of the hockey program forced the college's leadership to make a decision. Would it be basketball or hockey? One program had to go, and the logical choice was the more expensive of the two—hockey. So after nine seasons under just one head coach with a .595 winning percentage, SLU hockey after 1979 was no more.

St. Louis University Hockey Results

SEASON	CONFERENCE	RECORD	PCT.	LEAGUE FINISH	CONFERENCE TOURNAMENT	COACH
1970-74	Independent	9-19-2	.333	-	-	Bill Selman
1971-72	CCHA	15-15-3	.500	2nd	2nd	Bill Selman
1972-73	CCHA	27-11-0	.711	1st	2nd	Bill Selman
1973-74	CCHA	28-12-0	.700	2nd	1st	Bill Selman
1974-75	CCHA	26-13-1	.663	1st	1st	Bill Selman
1975-76	CCHA	24-15-2	.610	2nd	1st	Bill Selman
1976-77	CCHA	27-11-1	.705	1st	2nd	Bill Selman
1977-78	CCHA	21-17-2	.550	2nd	2nd	Bill Selman
1978-79	CCHA	16-16-3	.500	5th	-	Bill Selman
		193-129-14	.595			

Slapshots

★ ★

While the Saint Louis University Hockey Billikens no longer skate, Lindenwood University has become a hockey powerhouse with their men's and women's teams. Both teams have won championships in the American Collegiate Hockey Association, and both can now be seen playing at the NCAA Division I level at the Centene Community Ice Center in the St. Louis suburb of Maryland Heights.

There have been other forms of hockey entertainment, mainly played at the Family Arena in suburban St. Charles since its opening in 1999. One of the first teams to play there was the Missouri River Otters, a minor league hockey team in the United Hockey League. The team played under multiple ownership groups between 1999 and 2006. Probably the most interesting story within their tenure occurred during the NHL lockout in the 2004–05 season. With no NHL games to play, St. Louis Blues players Barret Jackman, Ryan Johnson, Bryce Salvador, and Jamal Mayers stayed in town and played for the Otters.

The St. Louis Vipers offered St. Louis hockey fans a different alternative: roller hockey. For six seasons beginning in 1993, the Vipers played initially at the St. Louis Arena and then moved to the new Kiel. At different times, former St. Louis Blues Bernie Federko and Perry Turbull would be behind the bench coaching the team. With a 74-53 record and a .541 winning percentage, the team was successful and would average almost 4,700 fans per game.

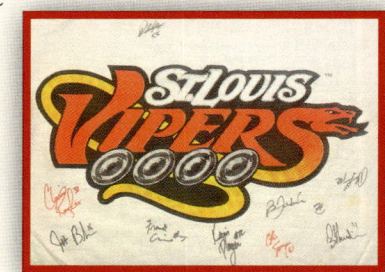

Barrett Jackman playing for the Otters
Courtesy of: Wikimedia Commons

Soccer

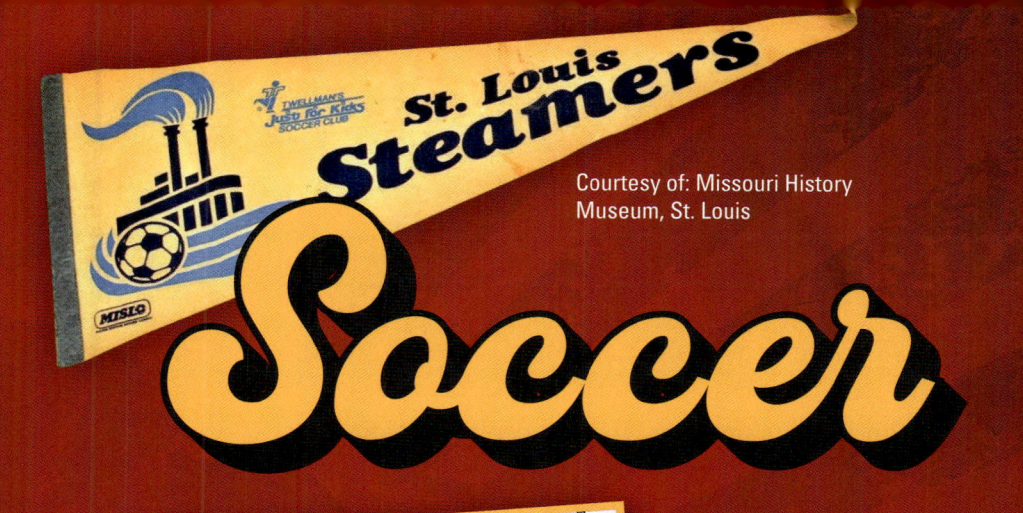

St. Louis Steamers

Courtesy of: Missouri History Museum, St. Louis

Four Hermann Trophy winners playing for the US National Team at Busch Stadium: Christen Press, Morgan Brian, Crystal Dunn and Kelley O'Hara. Courtesy of: Jim Wilson–MAC

St. Louis Stars Soccer Club

Courtesy of: Rich Noffke

Soccer Town

As with so many other sports, St. Louis has the reputation of being the "Soccer Capital" of North America due to its long and rich history within the sport. Today, cross-state Kansas City likes to lay claim to that title. Regardless of who makes the claim today, St. Louis's history always prevails. In fact, that history will soon expand when in 2023, the St. Louis City SC join Major League Soccer (MLS) and take the field in their newly constructed downtown stadium.

Soccer is an embedded element of St. Louis sports history due to the success of its amateur and professional teams. College teams from the region have won many national titles, with one alone having won more NCAA Division I titles than any other school in the nation. The city has hosted multiple professional teams over past decades to go along with the rich tradition of the city's youth soccer programs, which began within its large Catholic population, spurred by the many immigrants arriving in St. Louis with a rich soccer heritage. Decades ago, there was the saying among St. Louis children that the "publics" played baseball and football while the Catholic kids played soccer, and boy oh boy have they played.

Soccer legend Mia Hamm (a former Hermann Trophy winner) with winners Patrick Mullins and Crystal Dunn. Courtesy of: Jim Wilson–MAC

How prestigious is St. Louis in the eyes of the soccer world? Each January, the top college soccer players descend upon the Gateway City's Missouri Athletic Club (MAC) in downtown St. Louis. The MAC is host and presenter of the most coveted individual honor in NCAA Division I soccer, the Hermann Trophy. The trophy is presented annually to the top men's and women's college soccer players in the United States. It is college soccer's equivalent to college football's Heisman Trophy, and it is presented in St. Louis rather than New York due to the city's legacy.

The First Kicks to Greatness: Youth Soccer

A great sports tradition starts with the young, and that is truly the foundation of St. Louis's impressive soccer history. Youth soccer really began with, and was dominated by, the St. Louis Archdiocese's Catholic Youth Council (CYC) soccer programs. Decades before the CYC was formally organized, Catholic parish priests were forming leagues and teams. It became an inexpensive form of mass participation and recreation. Tennis legend Dwight Davis, who in 1912 was the City Park Commissioner, developed two fields to meet the needs of these teams. From there, soccer exploded across the city with the formation of the Muny Leagues in the years prior to 1941's formation of the CYC. A decade later, in 1951, the parish priest for St. Matthew's parish on the North Side organized the first women's soccer league to begin what would also be a decades-long run of dominance in women's soccer.

CYC Youth Soccer
Courtesy of: St. Louis CYC

With the region's youth playing soccer and clubs being formed, St. Louis would field teams that would soon achieve national distinction in US Open Cup and in National Amateur Cup play. For many, countless other victories lay ahead. The history of St. Louis amateur soccer is dotted

National Open Cup champion Simpkins at Sportsman's Park, 1950. Courtesy of: Frank Borghi

with teams named for their sponsors, including The Kensingtons, Stix, Baer & Fuller, the Ben Millers, Scullin Steel, and Simpkins-Ford.

Amateur soccer competitions have been around since the National Challenge Cup (later renamed the US Open Cup) was first presented in 1913 and followed by the National Amateur Cup's debut in 1923. St. Louis's amateur teams have raised the championship cups of these tournaments 22 times. Six St. Louis teams have hoisted the US Open Cup 10 different times (Stix, Baer & Fuller three times, St. Louis Kutis and St. Louis Simpkins-Ford twice each, and Ben Millers, St. Louis Busch Seniors, and St. Louis Scullin Steel once each).

St. Louis teams have also raised the National Amateur Cup 12 times and have been the runner-up another nine times. Three cups were won by a St. Louis Busch team and one by St. Louis Scott Gallagher. The St. Louis Kutis S. C. franchise provided eight more championships (one was in 1952, when they were named the St. Louis Raiders).

Without a doubt, those eight titles along with their two US Open Cup wins make Kutis the standout team throughout St. Louis's amateur soccer history. How dominating was the program? Between 1956 and 1961, Kutis won six consecutive National Amateur Cups—quite an impressive run for the team and the city they represented. In 1957, they pulled off the extremely difficult accomplishment of winning both the National Amateur and the US Open Cups.

While other cities in the post–World War II era drew and grew with urban migration, St. Louisans have always had a unique way of staying put. Local soccer players were no different. They stayed home and played and became the foundation for the city's incomparable collegiate soccer success.

Soccer's Title Town

★ ★

Colleges across the nation soon recognized St. Louis as a hotbed of soccer talent and began recruiting local athletes to their programs. Many, if not most, players chose to stay home and play for local schools here in "soccer town." No school in the country has a prouder soccer tradition than Saint Louis University. Led by coaches Bob Guelker and Harry Keough, who each won five titles at the helm, SLU leads all Division I Universities with their 10 National Titles (1959, '60, '62, '63, '65, '67, '69, '70, '72, and '73). How dominating was that? SLU won 10 of the NCAA's first 15 Division I National Championships since the tournament was first held in 1959. What is more amazing is the 1959 soccer team under Coach Guelker was the school's first season with soccer as a varsity sport. It would seem that all those amateur championships may have had a little to do with SLU's early success.

The handoff from Guelker to Harry Keough didn't disrupt SLU's dominance. Keough came with a résumé as one of St. Louis's greatest amateur players, including a World Cup and two Olympic appearances on top of winning two National Challenge Cups and seven National Amateur Cup titles. Keough began his coaching career at Florissant Valley Junior College before moving to SLU, where he recorded a dominating 213-50-23 coaching record.

SLU's First Varsity Soccer Team–1959
Courtesy of: Saint Louis University

In 1967, Bob Guelker left SLU and crossed the Mississippi River to begin and develop SIU–Edwardsville's (SIUE) soccer program. After five years playing as a nonconference independent program, SIUE joined the NCAA Division II ranks and won the first ever Division II National Championship Tournament in 1972, giving Guelker the distinction of winning each of the NCAA's top divisions' inaugural national championships. His SIUE program was on the road to national recognition. Guelker's teams would go on to be an NCAA Division I title runner-up in 1975 and then win the Division I National Championship in 1979. His combined coaching career would include seven national championships paired with two runners-up in a 311-77-26 record with SLU and SIUE from 1959 to 1985.

SIUE 1979 National Champions
Courtesy of: Southern Illinois University–Edwardsville collections

But St. Louis's championships kept coming. Under Coach Don Dallas, the St. Louis campus of the University of Missouri (UMSL) kept the NCAA Division II National Soccer Championship in the region for a second straight year. UMSL recorded an 11-0-3 season on their way to being crowned 1973's National Champions. Impressively, two of

The unbeaten University of Missouri–St. Louis Rivermen won the 1973 NCAA Division II national championship. The team went 11–0–3 in winning the only national title in any sport in UMSL's history. Courtesy of: University of Missouri–St. Louis.

98 | ST. LOUIS SPORTS MEMORIES

UMSL's ties were against SLU (Division I champion in both 1972 and 1973). Another tie came against the previous year's NCAA Division II National Champion, SIUE. St. Louis had definitely become college soccer's "title town."

But that's not even close to all of the titles. Coach Pete Sorber fielded a parallel soccer dynasty during his years at Florissant Valley Community College between 1967 and 1997. Harry Keough preceded Sorber at Florissant Valley before leaving to coach SLU after the 1966 season. Keough's last Florissant Valley team had been the runner up in the 1966 National Championship tournament.

But Sorber's tenure is beyond remarkable. With an impressive 415-85-22 record, he not only won 10 National Junior College Athletic Association (NJCAA) championships (1967, '69, '70, '71, '73, '75, '81, '84, '85, and '89), but his team was also the runner-up twice (1968 and '78) while winning 18 Regional

Florissant Valley's 1990 Women's National Championship was their second in three years.
Courtesy of: Karen Lombardo-Baker

titles. For six straight years between 1966 and 1971, the Florissant Valley men's soccer program was either the national champion or runner-up. Over a span of 24 seasons (1966–1989), they would appear in a National Championship game 13 times. Incredibly, in 23 seasons, the Florissant Valley men played in over 50 percent of the national title games.

Actually it was really 16 times in that span that Florissant Valley was a champion. Coach Karen Lombardo-Baker's women's team won the national title in 1988, was runner-up in 1989, and won the national crown once again in 1990. With her 1988 win, Lombardo-Baker became the first woman to win a NJCAA Women's National Championship, and she took home the NJCAA Coach of the Year award in both 1988 and 1990.

But again, that's not all. During those 23 years, the St. Louis Community College–Meramec men's soccer teams won the National Championship in 1972 and 1976 and were also the runner-up in 1973. Interestingly, in 1973, when they lost to Florissant Valley, it was the only time two St. Louis schools would play each other for the national championship.

Again, that was not all of the elite Junior College play in the region. Lewis & Clark Community College in Edwardsville was runner-up in the 1982 National Championship Game, and in the following year St. Louis Community College–Forest Park was the runner up. There would be only six seasons between 1966 and 1989 when a St. Louis program was not in the NJCAA Soccer National Championship game, a remarkable testament to the region's talent and coaching. The national titles kept coming. In 1991 and 1992, the St. Louis Community College–Meramec women's soccer teams won the NJCAA National Championship under Coach Jeff Karl. In 2016, the Washington University Women's Soccer team won a national title under Coach Jim Conlon. Add them all up, and you have 31 national college soccer championships between 1959 and 2016.

While most of the NJCAA players were from St. Louis, after their two-year careers were complete, many went on to star at SLU, SIUE, or other regional four-year programs. It is just a remarkable college soccer environment across the Gateway City that has left its footprints on many amateur programs as well as professional teams.

The Hill's Fab Four

★ ★

While the nation has looked in awe at the amateur ranks of St. Louis soccer, the greatest moment in the town's soccer history was a single game in June 1950. Some would say it was like something from a Hollywood movie. It was real, but the story was indeed later told on the silver screen. The 2005 film *The Game of Their Lives* chronicles the real-life story of the US World Cup team with six St. Louisans (five starters), four of whom had grown up together in the city's Italian neighborhood known as the Hill. Parts of the film were even shot in St. Louis. These men would forever be immortalized as part of the 1950 United States World Cup team that defeated England 1-0 in one of the

1950 US World Cup Team starting 11. Front row: Frank "Pee Wee" Wallace, Ed McIlvenny, Gino Pariani, Joe Gaetjens, John Souza, Ed Souza. Back row: Chubby Lyons (assistant coach), Joe Maca, Charlie Colombo, Frank Borghi, Harry Keough, Walter Bahr, Bill Jeffrey (coach). In addition to Wallace, Pariani, Colombo, Borghi and Keough, a sixth St. Louisan, Bob Annis, was on the team. Courtesy of: Frank Borghi Collection

FORGOTTEN TEAMS AND MOMENTS FROM AMERICA'S BEST SPORTS TOWN | 101

most momentous upsets in sports and World Cup history. How unlikely was a US win? *The New York Times* refused to print the score as it came off the wire just before their deadline to print because they thought it was a hoax.

Five starters—Frank Borghi (goalkeeper), Charley Colombo (center halfback), Harry Keough (right fullback), Gino Pariani (inside-right forward), and Frank "Pee Wee" Wallace (outside-right forward)—were joined by reserve defender Bob Annis, who did not play in the game against England. The St. Louisans were part of a 17-man squad coached by Penn State's Bill Jeffrey that had been quickly assembled just weeks before arriving as heavy underdogs in Belo Horizonte, a small, mountainous town in the World Cup's host country of Brazil. Their opponent was the poised and polished English team that had trained and played together for a significant period of time. On the other hand, the 500-to-1 longshot Americans were relative strangers to one another—except for Borghi, Colombo, Pariani, and Wallace, who had all grown up playing together on the Hill. The United States' Joe Gaetjens' 38th-minute header put the US ahead for keeps while the Hill's Borghi fended off all of the English shots. The upset was complete, and despite being ousted from the tournament by Chile 5-2, in their next game, the Americans had accomplished the unimaginable. The six St. Louisans came back to their hometown and went on with their lives. Their impossible story was being overshadowed in the news by North Korea's invasion of South Korea and President Truman's ordering of US troops into the conflict. Without the national fanfare that could have been, these players remain St. Louis heroes, and their names and moment forever etched in the city's soccer legacy.

Corner Kicks

★ ★

⭐ St. Louis has contributed at least one participant to each FIFA World Cup contested by the United States men's team.

⭐ The "Bronze Boot" (a.k.a. the Joseph Carenza, Sr. Perpetual Trophy) series was played almost annually between SLU and SIUE from 1971 to 1998 during the period of the two teams' dominance of college soccer. NCAA scheduling regulations ended the rivalry for a few decades until its return in recent years. SLU has dominated the series with a 21-5-1 record.

Courtesy of: Saint Louis University collection

⭐ The Bronze Boot game has drawn record-setting crowds. The October 30, 1980, game held at Busch Stadium II broke the NCAA soccer attendance record (set in 1973, also here in St. Louis) with a new record of 22,512 soccer fans that still stands today.

⭐ The 1981 women's team at the University of Missouri–St. Louis was the first major-college women's soccer team in St. Louis and played in the first-ever US women's national college soccer tournament. The Riverwomen went 16–0–0 until losing in the national semifinals and then in the third-place game to finish fourth.

⭐ In 2005, the MISL's St. Louis Steamers acquired the playing rights to female forward Lindsay Kennedy. The Harris-Stowe State College grad became the first female to play in the MISL when she took the field in February 2005.

⭐ Lori Chalupny is considered the finest women's player developed in St. Louis and starred for St. Louis Athletica during the club's brief tenure in Women's Professional Soccer. She also captained the US women's National Team.

St. Louis Soccer Goes Pro: Stars I

★ ★

As with almost every other sport, they begin and gain a following with a successful amateur program long before the evolution of professional teams. With a strong and successful amateur presence, it was only natural that professional soccer would take off in the Gateway City.

The St. Louis Stars were the first. In 1967, they joined nine other teams in the newly founded National Professional Soccer League (NPSL). Owned by Bob Hermann (after whom the Hermann Trophy is named) and Bill Bidwill (NFL Cardinals), the Stars played their games in Busch Stadium II. Even though St. Louis was producing the country's best college players, the Stars inaugural team was composed of players from nine different countries, including nine from Yugoslavia alone.

The league even had a television contract with CBS to televise its games nationally. An additional oddity of the league was its standings point system, which would be adopted later in other professional soccer leagues. Teams would get six points for a win, three for a draw, none for a loss, and one bonus point for each of the first three goals scored.

In the league's only year of existence, coach George Mihaljevic's St. Louis Stars finished second in the Western Division, 29 points behind the NPSL Champion Oakland Clippers. They played their first game against the Chicago Spurs on April 16. The team's leading scorer was Germany's Rudi Kölbl with 15 goals. Not surprisingly with the town's love of soccer, the Stars' 7,613 average attendance was the highest in the league. In an interesting concept, the NPSL had a runner-up game played in conjunction with the two division winners' championship game. In the runner-up game the Stars defeated the Philadelphia Spartans at home and earned a berth in the Commissioner's Cup game the following week at Busch Stadium II against the NPSL champion Oakland Clippers, who bested the Stars by a score of 6-3.

The 1967 National Professional Soccer League Results

EASTERN DIVISION	GAMES	WINS	LOSSES	TIES
Baltimore Bays	32	14	9	9
Philadelphia Spartans	32	14	9	9
New York Generals	32	11	13	8
Atlanta Chiefs	31	10	12	9
Pittsburgh Phantoms	31	10	14	7

WESTERN DIVISION	GAMES	WINS	LOSSES	TIES
Oakland Clippers	32	19	8	5
St. Louis Stars	32	14	11	7
Chicago Spurs	32	10	11	11
Toronto Falcons	32	10	17	5
Los Angeles Toros	32	7	15	10

St. Louis Soccer Goes Pro: Stars II

★ ★

After the 1967 season, the NPSL merged with the United Soccer Association to form the North American Soccer League (NASL). The Stars joined 16 other teams to play a 32-game schedule in 1968. While averaging 5,388 fans per game (much higher than the league average), coach Rudi Gutendorf's 1968 Stars finished third in their division with a 12-6-14 record and did not make the playoffs. Germany's Rudi Kölbl would once again be the Star's leading scorer with 15 goals.

The 1968 St. Louis Stars. Front row, from left: Pat McBride, Cheung Chi-Doy, Joe Fuhrmann, Casey Frankiewicz, Carl Gentile, Willi Wrenger, Kay Wiestal. Back row: Manager Rudy Gutendorf, Nick Krat, Mike Kalicanin, Don Ceresia, Rudy Kolbl, Barney Vidinic, Joe Puls, Norb Pogrzeba, Jack Kineally, Eddie Clear, and trainer Steve Middleman. Courtesy of: Mary Weidiner Collection

The next year would turn out be a financially turbulent season. There would be no national television contract in 1969. Only five teams would still be around for a 16-game schedule. All teams began cutting back on player salaries and were thus attracting lesser talent. Critics said the league was becoming nothing more than a fancy semi-pro league.

Bob Kehoe would coach the Stars for the next two seasons beginning in 1969. He had captained the 1965 US National Team and would become the first American-born coach in the NASL (the start of a trend). Kazimierz "Casey" Frackiewics, a retired Polish player who had come to the Stars the year before, was the team's All-Star selection and led the Stars with 16 goals. The results weren't any better, as the team's record fell to 3-2-11 for fourth place before an average 2,274 fans.

The diminishing fans in the stands were becoming lost in the confines of Busch Stadium II, so the team moved to Washington University's Francis Field to start the new decade. They moved back to Busch Stadium in 1971 as the crowds increased, but would return to Francis Field in 1975. They also started fielding more Americans and especially local players. Future Hall of Famer and St. Louisan Pat McBride emerged as a 1970 All-Star and led the team in goals that year. After third- and fourth-place finishes in 1970 and '71, the team won their division in 1972. It would be their best finish, but they would

Courtesy of: Missouri History Museum, St. Louis

lose to the New York Cosmos 2-1 in the league finals. Winning did attract fans, and the Stars' average attendance of 7,773 again led the league. Signing home-grown and American talent kept the fans coming, and the Stars would continue to average over 6,000 fans for the next five years as the team remained competitive. Behind the NASL's Coach of the Year John Sewell, who was actually a player-coach, the Stars would win their division in 1975 after signing England's Peter Bonetti to solidify the goalkeeper position. As in past years, the playoffs were not kind, and the Stars lost to the Portland Timbers in the semifinals.

Despite good players like All-Stars Pat McBride, John Sewell, Peter Bonetti, Al Trost, and Ray Evans, the Stars could not put together a winning season in their last two years (1976 and '77). So after the 1977 season, the ownership group took the famous advice of newspaper editor Horace Greeley to "go west." The team was moved to Anaheim, California, and became the California Surf. Many of the stars made the trip and stayed with the team until it dissolved in 1981. Outdoor soccer would be put on a pause in St. Louis.

St. Louis Stars II Results

YEAR	WINS	LOSSES	TIES	DIVISION FINISHES	PLAYOFFS	AVG ATTEND.
1968	12	6	14	3rd	NA	5,388
1969	3	2	11	4th	NA	2,274
1970	5	2	17	3rd	NA	2,745
1971	6	5	13	4th	NA	3,579
1972	7	3	4	1st	Runners-up	7,773
1973	7	5	7	2nd	NA	6,337
1974	4	1	15	4th	NA	7,374
1975	13	9	-	1st	Semifinals	6,071
1976	5	19	-	5th	NA	6,150
1977	12	14	-	2nd	First round	9,794
TOTAL	74	66	81			

Pele

★ ★ ★ ★ ★ ★ ★ ★ ★ ★ ★ ★ ★ ★ ★ ★ ★ ★ ★

One high point of the 1968 season that became a piece of St. Louis soccer history took place at Busch Stadium II on June 30, when the Stars played an exhibition game against Santos of Brazil—bringing soccer's greatest superstar, Pele, to St. Louis for the first time. Pele would later play against the Stars for the New York Cosmos from 1975 to 1977.

The June 30 game was played on a hot Sunday afternoon before 20,116 fans. The temperature in the seats exceeded 95 degrees and was much higher on the field. The sun and heat kept many fans away and impacted the players as well. The Brazilians played their games at home in the evening and were not used to playing in the heat of the day. The Stars Casey Frackiewics' two goals had given the Stars the lead before the visitors came back to tie the game. The St. Louisans hung tough all game with the score tied at 2 heading into the later stages of the game. The Stars and their fans were even looking for a possible win when in the closing minutes Pele put the ball into the net for a Santos win. Despite the loss, it was definitely a memorable St. Louis soccer moment, as the fans got the chance to see one of the greatest in the game.

Courtesy of: Missouri History Museum, St. Louis

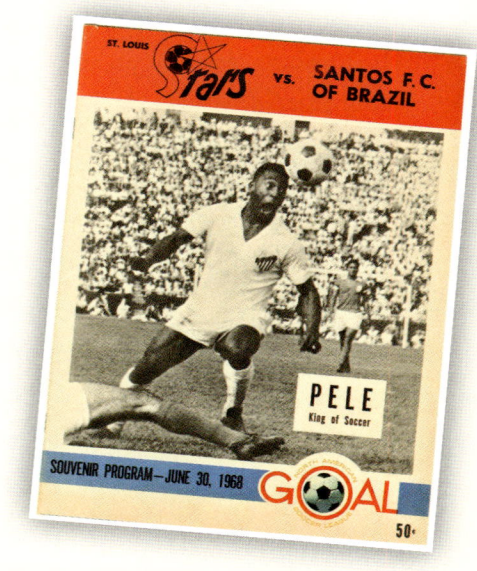

FORGOTTEN TEAMS AND MOMENTS FROM AMERICA'S BEST SPORTS TOWN | **109**

Soccer Goes Indoors

It would be nearly three decades before professional soccer would once again be played outdoors in St. Louis after the Stars folded in 1977. The movement indoors had actually begun during the Stars tenure. Professional indoor soccer in St. Louis began in March 1971 when the St. Louis Stars hosted the NASL Professional Hoc-Soc Tournament at the St. Louis Arena. It was a four-team tournament won by the Dallas Tornado. The Stars would win the third-place consolation game.

In 1975, the Stars participated in a 16-team indoor tournament hosted by the NASL, but the team did not make it to the semi-finals. The next year, the NASL once again held an indoor tournament for its 12 teams and once again, the Stars could not advance.

Even though the Stars were not advancing in the tournaments, indoor soccer was proving to be a success. On February 13, 1974, 12,241 fans packed the Arena to see the Stars host the Moscow Red Army team. After winning in Toronto and Philadelphia, the Russians came to town to close their three-city North American tour in convincing fashion. The Stars initially held the lead for a brief 11 seconds before the Russians turned it on and administered an 11-4 shellacking. The Stars' Denny Vaninger was the only one who could crack the Russian defense, scoring all four St. Louis goals. While the Stars' indoor results weren't that pretty over the years, the precedent was set for the indoor game, and the fans showed they would come.

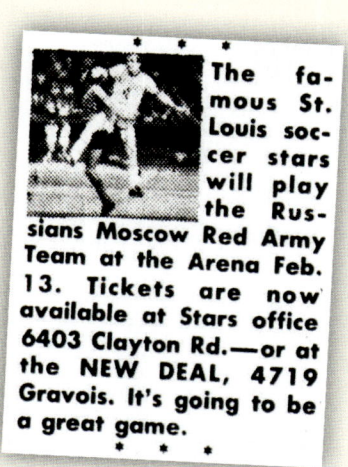

The famous St. Louis soccer stars will play the Russians Moscow Red Army Team at the Arena Feb. 13. Tickets are now available at Stars office 6403 Clayton Rd.—or at the NEW DEAL, 4719 Gravois. It's going to be a great game.

"Steamin'" in the Arena

★ ★ ★ ★ ★ ★ ★ ★ ★ ★ ★ ★ ★

The St. Louis Steamers came to town for a somewhat successful nine-year indoor soccer run. They joined the Major Indoor Soccer League (MISL) in 1979. The MISL had begun play in the fall of 1978. Indoor soccer was becoming more than just the action on the field. Mirroring the fast-paced video age of the 1980s, it became a total entertainment package where the fans in the stands were entertained with booming music, smoke machines, and loud and dramatic pronouncements over the loudspeakers.

The Steamers would join the league in its second year and would be staffed with local talent and interesting ownership groups over the years. The team was owned by a partnership led by Stan Musial from 1980 to 1983 and by baseball executive Bing Devine from 1987 to 1988. The Steamers would play at the St. Louis Arena and were so popular they would, for four seasons beginning in 1980, outdraw the team they shared the facility with—the

Courtesy of: Missouri History Museum, St. Louis

FORGOTTEN TEAMS AND MOMENTS FROM AMERICA'S BEST SPORTS TOWN | 111

NHL's Blues. In the 1981–82 season alone, the Steamers would average 17,107 fans per game compared to the Blues' average of 14,433.

At their first home opener on December 14, 1979, over 18,000 fans came to see winning soccer and local faces. The Steamers' strategy was to use the talent coming out of the area's winning local schools. While they didn't make the playoffs in their first season, they would win their division and make it to the MISL finals in each of the next two seasons (1980–81 and 1982–83) only to lose to Steve Zungul and the New York Arrows.

Zungul was an MISL machine. He was the MISL Most Valuable Player six times, the Scoring Champion six times, and the Pass Master (most assists) four times, while playing on eight championship-winning teams (and one runner-up). He was the MISL's all-time leader in goals, assists, and points. For Steamer fans, it was like the Browns baseball fans

1980–81 Steamers. Front, from left: Steve Sullivan, Winston Hackett, Emilio Romero, Tony Glavin, John Stremlau, and Dan McDonnell. Middle row: equipment manager George Hanheide, Yilmaz Orhan, Jeff Sendobry, Sam Bick, Greg Makowski, Ty Keough, Tony Bellinger, and trainer Bill Jennings. Back row: Assistant Coach Tim Rooney, Steve Pecher, Don Ebert, Greg Villa, Eric Delabar, Manny Schwartz, Slobo Ilijevski, Denny Vaninger, Emilio John, Carl Rose, and Coach Pat McBride. Courtesy of: John Stremlau

who came to watch Babe Ruth play when the Yankees came to town or for Cardinal fans who would come out to watch Willie Mays when the Giants were the visitors.

The playoff soccer jinx of the Stars would continue. The Steamers would make the playoffs the next four years and would even make it to the finals again in the 1983–84 season, when they lost to Baltimore. In their last two seasons (1986–87 and 1987–88), they failed to make the playoffs, and average attendance was down to 6,440 in the last year. Their last game would be on April 15, 1988. The Steamers and several other franchises then folded after the season.

The team was .500 or better in five of their nine seasons and made the playoffs six times. Their average attendance significantly outpaced the league's average. The team had star-quality coaches in Pat McBride (Coach of the Year in 1979–80), Al Trost, Dave Clements, and Tony Glavin. They had a Rookie of the Year in Don Ebert and All-Stars Steve Pecher, Tony Glavin, Slobo Ilijevski, and Sam Bick rounding out a roster with Dan Counce and Tom Galanti. As with so many other sports franchises in St. Louis and across America, success was elusive and their tenure was not long—just nine seasons. They played their last game on April 15, 1988. After the 1987–88 season, the team ceased operations, and the MISL terminated the franchise.

St. Louis Steamers Results

YEARS	RECORD	STL AVE ATTENDANCE	MISL AVE ATTENDANCE
1979–80	12-20	14,060	6,102
1980–81	25-15	15,219	6,839
1981–82	28-16	17,107	8,735
1982–83	26-22	14,693	7,895
1983–84	26-22	13,992	8,868
1984–85	24-24	12,711	8,696
1985–86	23-25	10,189	8,680
1986–87	19-33	7,038	8,714
1987–88	18-38	6,440	8,439
TOTALS	201-215		

Stormed

★ ★

There was a whole lost season for St. Louis soccer fans at the Arena after the Steamers folded in 1988. The St. Louis Storm joined the MISL for the 1989–90 season. Serbian born Milan Mandaric, a wealthy soccer fan from Yugoslavia who had achieved financial success in Silicon Valley, declined a chance to purchase the Steamers in 1988. Instead, he wanted his own team with its own brand and a fresh start. He won a MISL expansion bid to bring the game back to St. Louis. Looking for a quick impact, Mandaric brought fellow Serb Don Popovic in to coach the club. Popovic had plenty of MISL experience, having taken the New York Arrows to the MISL's first four titles (1979–1982).

**1990-1991
ST. LOUIS STORM
SCHEDULE**

**LIGHTNING
STRIKES
OCTOBER 19th**

Mandaric and Popovic had less than 100 days to put their team in order after winning the bid. At the same time, the Los Angeles Lazers dropped out of the league and the Storm was awarded the first five picks in the Lazers' dispersal draft, which yielded fan favorites from the Steamers, Daryl Doran and Slobodan Ilijevski.

The Storm's first season was disappointing; they finished with a 24-28 record before getting booted from the playoffs in the first round against the eventual MISL Champions, the San Diego Sockers. Over the course of the season, the team had lost $1.5 million, which led Mandaric to consider folding operations. But a group of local investors came on board to help shore up the team. Popovic did his part as well by bringing in some "Slavic firepower" with the signing of winger Predrag Radosavljevic, a.k.a. "Preki," for the team's second season in 1990. Preki was called the Michael Jordan of the MISL. He contributed 68 goals and 53 assists alongside Thompson Usiyan, who added 64 goals for the Storm. The team finished the 1990–91 season with a

32–20 record, second best in the eight-team league. Despite the record, the city's soccer playoff jinx continued as the Storm was once again bounced from the playoffs by the Sockers in the semifinal round. One positive from the season was the team's league-leading average attendance of 7,772 fans per game, which helped keep the team's losses manageable.

Initially, the 1991–92 season looked promising. Popovic had flipped Usiyan for one of his former Arrows, star Branko Sergota. But luck was not on the Storm's side. It turned out not to be a good move or season. Goalie Zoltan Toth, who had been so good the year before, was injured and abruptly retired two games into the season. With a record of 12-20 heading into the season's final month, Popovic was fired. The Storm finished in last place in the seven-team league with a record of 17-23. Despite the poor performance, fans continued to come to the Arena, and the Storm increased their league-leading average attendance to 10,266 fans per game. Despite the losing season, the team even set an attendance record for the final game of the season on April 3 with 16,959 fans. It would be the team's last game.

Mandaric was losing interest in St. Louis and focusing on the expensive new arena being built in his Silicon Valley hometown of San Jose. Like the Storm, other teams were in trouble, and by July 1992, the MISL was no more as team after team began to fold.

St. Louis Storm's Results

YEARS	STORM'S RECORD	STORM'S AVE ATTENDANCE	MISL AVE ATTENDANCE
1989–90	24-28	6,848	7,765
1990–91	32-20	7,722	6,566
1991–92	17-23	10,266	7,844
TOTALS	73-71		

Ambushed

★★★★★★★★★★★★★★★★★★★★

As the St. Louis Storm weathered their losing season in 1992, urologist Dr. Abraham Hawatmeh began efforts to acquire the team from Mandaric. St. Louis was still the attendance leader, but a cheaper cost model was needed for success. Hawatmeh had become a minority owner in the club a year earlier. As the team was sliding, he refrained from investing in the team's financial "storm."

With the Storm and MISL gone in July 1992, Hawatmeh and his investors quickly jumped in over the next month and purchased the National Professional Soccer League's (NPSL) Tulsa Ambush for a move to St. Louis. The NPSL had been formed under the moniker the American Indoor Soccer Association in 1984 before updating its name in 1990. The NPSL operated with a lower cost structure than the MISL, which would keep the new league solvent through 2001.

Courtesy of: Missouri History Museum, St. Louis

One of the interesting concepts of the NPSL was their scoring system that awarded goals worth 1, 2, or 3 points depending upon distance or game situation. Hoping that large crowds would show up, the team initially played in the Arena before moving to the new Kiel Center in 1994. To ensure a strong following, the team was formed around the region's local talent.

Once they began play on November 6, 1992, the Ambush rewarded their fans with good play. The first season didn't quite turn out as planned. They lost more than they won before turning it all around in the 1993–94 season under new coach Daryl Doran. After winning their division with a 25-15 record, the Ambush fell three games to one to the

Cleveland Crunch in the NPSL Championship Game. The team built on that loss, winning their division the next year and bringing home St. Louis's first professional soccer championship with a four-game sweep of the Harrisburg Heat to culminate the 1994–95 season.

The next season, the Ambush fell to third place in their division and lost in the Division Finals. They would bounce back and win their division each of the next three years. They would lose in the Conference Finals in the 1996–97 season and then make it to the NPSL Finals in the 1997–98 and 1998–99 seasons, but they would lose each time. They were beaten by the Milwaukee Wave in the first final and then the Cleveland Crunch in the next. The Ambush had appeared in four NPSL Finals in six years, but only won it all once. They had given St. Louis soccer fans consistently high-quality play, but the tide would quickly change.

The 1999–2000 season would be the Ambush's last. It was a season filled with defections and uncertainty. Star player-coach Daryl Doran, the past NPSL Defender-of-the Year Kevin Hundelt, and the team's top scoring threat Mark Moser left the team along with some key members of the team's front office prior to the season. The team would go 11-33 and miss the playoffs for the first time in eight years. Year over year attendance fell from 8,472 to 4,668 per game, a 44 percent drop in fans coming through the turnstile. To make matters worse, the management of the St. Louis Blues, with whom the team shared the Kiel Center, declined a lease extension for the Ambush. The team decided to take a leave of absence for the 2000–01 season, but they would never return, and two seasons later the NPSL would cease to exist.

St. Louis Ambush Results

YEARS	RECORD	ATTENDANCE
1992-93	19-21	7,718
1993-94	25-15	8,143
1994-95	30-10	7,881
1995-96	24-16	9,102
1996-97	27-13	9,072
1997-98	27-13	8,203
1998-99	21-19	8,472
1999-00	11-33	4,668
TOTALS	184-140	

Same Name, Different League: The "New" Steamers

So what happened to Ambush players Doran, Hundelt, and Moser prior to the 1999–00 season? A rival soccer league lured them away. The World Indoor Soccer League (WISL) had formed in 1998, and an expansion franchise was awarded to a new team with an old name: the St. Louis Steamers that would begin play during the 2000–01 season in the new Family Arena.

Daryl Doran would be the first coach of the "new" Steamers. They went 9-15, placing fifth in 2000–01, and then 11-13 while placing third the next year. Despite losing records, soccer fans continued coming out as the Steamers posted an average attendance of 5,398 per game the first year and 4,812 the next. As the calendar turned to the 2002–03 season, the WISL merged with the Major Indoor Soccer League (MISL II). Organizational issues kept the Steamers out of the merged league for a year. They rejoined the league for the 2003–04 season going 14-22 (third place) and 20-20 (fourth place) the following year. That slight improvement in wins put them on the path to a first-place finish in the 2005–06 season with a 23-7 record, but they lost the MISL Championship match to the Baltimore Blast. It was the high-water mark for the team, and it would also be their last season. Even as they were starting to win on the field, the Steamers, like so many other teams in professional indoor soccer, could not overcome the financial obstacles that would put them out of business after the 2005–06 season.

St. Louis Steamers WISL Results

YEARS	RECORD	ATTENDANCE
2000	9-15	5,391
2001	11-13	4,812
2002-03	Did Not Play	
2003-04	14-22	3,483
2004-05	20-20	4,794
2005-06	23-7	5,675
TOTALS	77-77	

Leagues Come, Leagues Go

Indoor Professional soccer in St. Louis has had a roller-coaster history of ups and downs. There had been four indoor teams over a 26-year period that yielded just one professional championship. The early outdoor pro teams fared no better. Yet, in all those years, St. Louisans turned out in record fashion, filling the seats at their home venues in far higher numbers than their rivals. Soccer has always been in the blood of St. Louis fans, and they have always showed it.

There have been continued attempts for new teams with new league startups. The list is actually quite long. There was the St. Louis Knights attempt in 1994 as an outdoor team that lasted only two seasons. The St. Louis Strikers came in 2003 and went in 2004 while playing in the United Soccer Leagues' Premier Development League at St. Louis Soccer Park. Then there were the St. Louis Archers of the Women's Premier Soccer League on the SIUE campus that lasted just four seasons between 2004 and 2007.

Courtesy of: St. Louis Athletica

In 2009, the St. Louis Athletica was awarded a charter franchise into the Women's Professional Soccer League. The team opened up in SIUE's stadium before moving across the river to Fenton's Soccer Park. It was a team with a lot of potential and well-known stars led by US Olympic and World Cup players Lori Chalupny and Hope Solo. They went 10-7-4 in their first year, placing second in the league before being bounced from the playoffs. The team started the 2010 season and folded after just three games for financial reasons.

Over the next decade, there would be multiple attempts at professional soccer. One of the longest-lasting has been the reincarnated St. Louis Ambush, who began play in 2013 as part of the Major Indoor Soccer League (MISL) in the area's Family Arena. Daryl Doran coached the inaugural team to a sixth-place finish. After the season, the Ambush, along with five other teams, left the MISL to join the Major Arena Soccer League (MASL), where they still play today. The franchise's 48-114 record is reflective of five coaching changes and constant roster turnover. In the 2021 season, when several teams did not play due to the COVID pandemic, the Ambush finally made it to the playoffs but lost in the quarterfinals to the Kansas City Comets. With the lack of wins and decreasing attendance, the Ambush face an uncertain future. The birth and the success of the St. Louis SC will either increase soccer interest and aid the Ambush, or it will pull fans away and spur the demise of the team. Time will tell.

St. Louis City SC will kick off their inaugural season in Major League Soccer (MLS) in 2023 as an expansion team in Centene Stadium, a new multi-million dollar downtown stadium built specifically for the team. The team is led by the first female-majority ownership team in the MLS under Caroline Kindle Betz. They are driven to restore St. Louis's soccer greatness. Here's hoping the spirit of St. Louis soccer and its fans will rally and support this new team for many years and many victories.

St. Louis Ambush Results

YEARS	LEAGUE	RECORD	AVE ATTENDANCE
2013-14	MISL	4-16	5,636
2014-15	MASL	8-12	6,110
2015-16	MASL	5-15	5,301
2016-17	MASL	1-19	2,574
2017-18	MASL	3-19	2,605
2018-19	MASL	10-14	2,553
2019-20	MASL	9-12	3,096
2020-21	MASL	8-7	1,758
2021-22	MASL	10-12-2	3,327
TOTALS		58-116-2	3,551

Golf

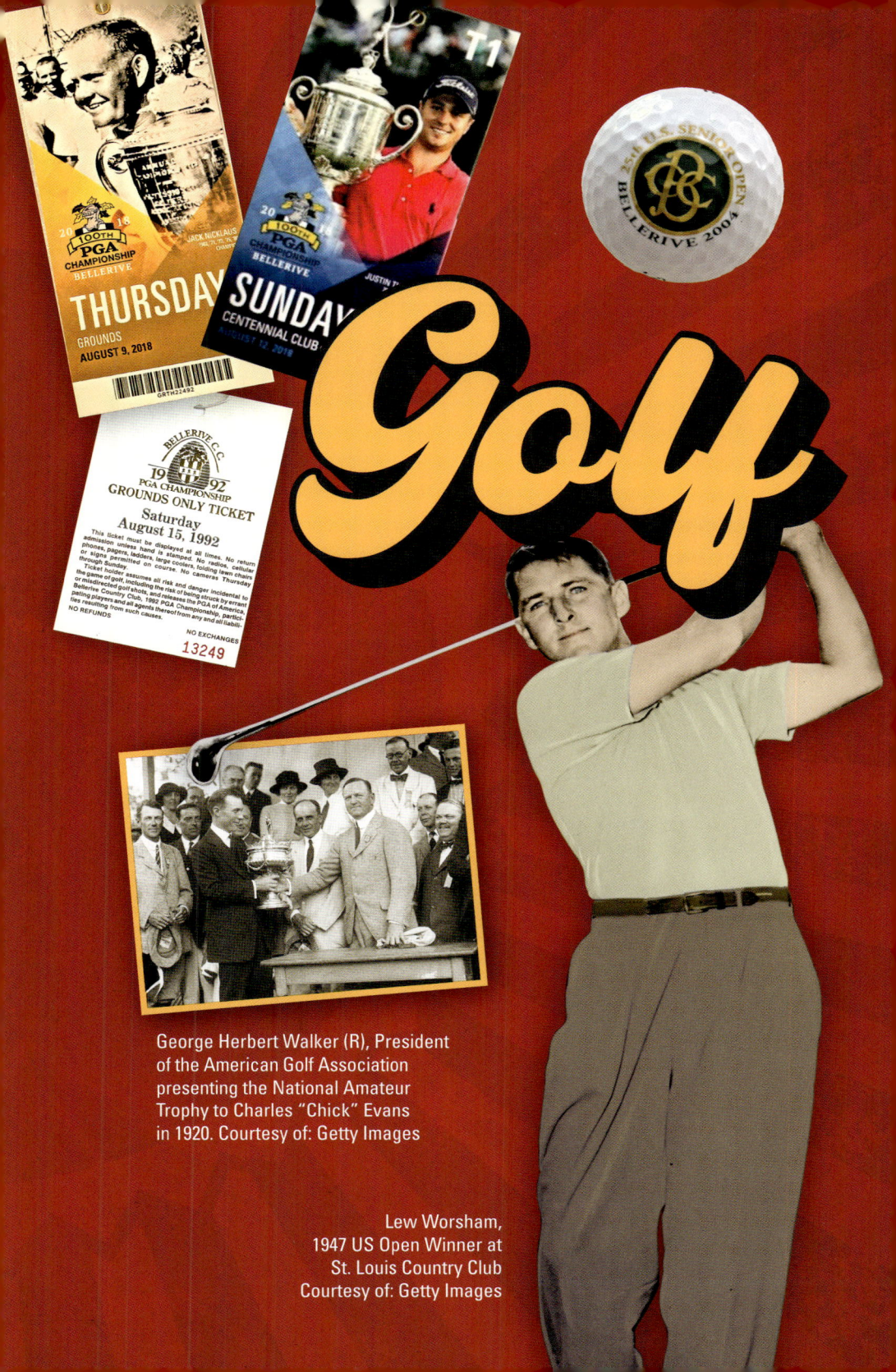

George Herbert Walker (R), President of the American Golf Association presenting the National Amateur Trophy to Charles "Chick" Evans in 1920. Courtesy of: Getty Images

Lew Worsham, 1947 US Open Winner at St. Louis Country Club
Courtesy of: Getty Images

The Sport of Gentlemen Arrives

★ ★

Long known as the sport of gentleman, golf has a rich history in St. Louis. It began decades before Glen Echo hosted the first golf matches in Olympic play in 1904. St. Louisans have been nurtured over the years on the history of the game while witnessing some of the most recent special moments on the sport's pro tour.

Scottish immigrants helped spur and even design many of the sport's first courses as the game began to grow in popularity during the late 1800s. The city's wealthier collegians were returning home after their years of study back East, and they wanted to continue playing the game they had taken up. This led to the eventual development of many of the area's local courses for the affluent set on the grounds of numerous prestigious country clubs across the metropolitan area.

But it was not just a rich man's (or woman's) game. Public courses would begin springing up for those of more modest means as well. Stretched between Glen Echo (1901) and Norwood Hills (1922) Country Clubs in St. Louis's northern suburbs, Normandie Golf Club opened in 1901, and today is the oldest public golf course west of the Mississippi River. There was a time when these three entities were joined by another exclusive private club: Bellerive Country Club.

Glen Echo Country Club 1901
Courtesy of: Wikimedia Commons

122 | ST. LOUIS SPORTS MEMORIES

Bellerive had formed in 1897 and relocated in 1910 to expanded grounds within close proximity to these other courses. Today, the fairways and paths of Bellerive are not walked by golfers but instead by students of the University of Missouri–St. Louis going to class. In the late 1950s, Bellerive's grounds were sold as the club moved west following shifting population patterns and settled in the St. Louis suburb of Town and Country.

The same story can be told for the development and location of St. Louis (1892) and Old Warson (1955) Country Clubs, which first developed on the transportation lines in the open fields of the tony enclave of Ladue. In 1910, the Busch family of the beer dynasty began an effort to establish a private club in the undeveloped area southwest of St. Louis that eventually evolved into Sunset Country Club, which features the finest golf course in that part of the metropolitan area.

Over the decades, private and public courses have sprung up and fallen along with the region's population shifts. Some were owned by suburban cities like Florissant or University City, but two of the longest-running courses also date back to the 1904 World's Fair period and are laid out in one of the largest city parks in the nation.

The Forest Park Golf Course, formally titled the Norman K. Probstein Golf Course, opened in 1912. This course, open to the public, offers 27 holes that wind through the western boundaries of Forest Park. The Highlands Golf and Tennis Center, formerly known as the St. Louis Amateur Athletic Association course or AAA for short, was established in the southeastern edge of Forest Park to provide low-cost athletic facilities to the community. Over the years, it has spurred the sporting careers of many local athletes. St. Louisan and LPGA legend Judy Rankin got her start playing on this course. For decades, these links provided the only course open to African Americans across the region.

All of these golf courses form the foundation of St. Louis's esteemed golf history, where many players learned and mastered the game and where greatness was displayed for the city's fans.

The Big Boys Tee Off

★ ★ ★ ★ ★ ★ ★ ★ ★ ★ ★ ★ ★ ★ ★ ★ ★ ★

Historically, golf fans have not always associated St. Louis with the tour's big-name courses and events such as those at Augusta, Doral, Pebble Beach, or Torrey Pines. But in recent years, that has changed. St. Louis has captured the attention of the golf world with repeated large turnouts and dramatic finishes. St. Louis has quietly built up a very impressive résumé of dramatic moments involving some of the greatest players in the history of the game.

That history really starts in June 1947 when the first major tournament, the 47th US Open, came to town and was played at St. Louis Country Club. It would also be the first locally televised US Open and would further stir St. Louisans' interest in the game. Lew Worsham would win that year's Open for the 17th consecutive major championship won by an American-born golfer. His share of the winnings was $2,000, but his victory did not come without a fight. It took an 18-hole, one-stroke playoff win over Sam Snead, which would contribute to legendary golfer Snead's string of four runners-up without ever winning the Open.

Right on heels of the 1947 Open, the PGA showed up in town the following spring for the 30th PGA Championship at Norwood Hills Country Club in May 1948. In what would be his second and final PGA Championship, Ben Hogan won the match play championship 7 & 6 over Mike Turnesa. The match play format called for 12 rounds (216 holes) in seven days. To get to the finals, Hogan defeated Jimmy Demaret in the semifinal round while Turnesa defeated

Ben Hogan 1948 PGA
Courtesy of: Getty Images

Claude Harmon in the semis after defeating Sam Snead in the quarterfinals. Hogan took $3,500 home with the win and became the third of six players in golfing history to win the US Open and the PGA Championship in the same calendar year. Gene Sarazen (1922), Walter Hagen (1924), Jack Nicklaus (1980), Tiger Woods (2000), and Brooks Koepka (2018) were the only others. Like Hogan, Koepka got one of his two titles in St. Louis.

It would be almost two decades before another major returned to St. Louis when Bellerive Country Club hosted the 65th US Open in June 1965. Like the previous Open, this would also end in a playoff. With the longest course (7,191 yards) to date in Open play, Bellerive offered the 150 players a little bit of a challenge, and it would take an

Gary Player US Open 1965
Courtesy of: Getty Images

additional 18 holes in a playoff round before South Africa's Gary Player would defeat Australia's Kel Nagel by three strokes and take home $26,000. While it was Player's only Open title, the win completed the 29-year-old's career Grand Slam. The world got to see the best of St. Louis, as this was the first Open to be televised in color. Perhaps the most memorable moment may have come after it was all over. Gary Player donated his entire winnings to junior golf ($20,000), cancer research ($5,000), and to his caddy ($2,000; $1,000 of the purse and $1,000 of his own money). Player reasoned that he wanted to thank the people of the United States as well as fight the disease that had taken his mother when he was eight years old.

In September 1971, the world once more came back to St. Louis as Old Warson Country Club hosted the 19th Ryder Cup. The Ryder Cup is a golf match between teams from Europe and the United States that takes place every other year. The venue alternates as well between courses in Europe and the US. For the first time in the event's history, the tournament would take place in St. Louis. A 12-man team with the likes of Jack Nicklaus, Arnold Palmer, and Lee Trevino faced a team from Great Britain. A total of 16½ points are needed to win the Cup out of the 32 possible points to be gained over the three-day event. The crowd cheered the United States to a Cup win with 18½ points versus Great Britain's 13½.

By August 1992, it had been over four decades since the PGA was last played in St. Louis. Its return would mark the second major to be played at Bellerive Country Club, which had hosted the US Open in 1965. Zimbabwe's Nick Price would take home $280,000 in the first of what would be three major championships. The win was by a margin of three strokes ahead of runners-up John Cook, Nick Faldo, Jim Gallagher, and Gene Sauers.

Nicklaus and Palmer
1971 Ryder Cup
Courtesy of: Getty Images

When the centennial PGA Championship came once more to Bellerive Country Club in August 2018, the St. Louis community showed an international television audience what an outstanding golf town the Gateway City is. Once again, huge crowds showed up and followed the golfers along Bellerive's expanded course, and they weren't disappointed. Brooks Koepka won the event (his third major) by two strokes over a charging Tiger. While many remember the dangerous thunderstorms that suspended the

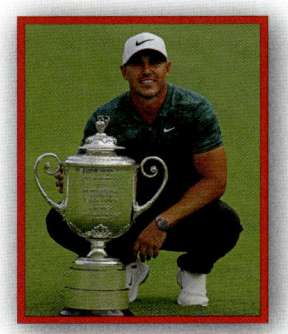

Brooks Koepka at the
2018 PGA championship
Courtesy of: Getty Images

second-round matches with over half the golfers still on the course, there would be a fascinating crescendo the next day as many golfers not only had to play the third round but also finish the second. Play began at 7 a.m. the next day and would continue toward an amazing finish the next evening.

The 2018 Championship marked a comeback for Tiger Woods, who had suffered through a series of back surgeries between 2015 and 2018 that allowed him to play in only one tournament between August 2015 and January 2018. As Tiger found his former greatness at Bellerive, the crowd was behind him with every swing. Koepka, however, was not letting up under the pressure of Tiger's charge. He shot a 66 in the third round and held a 4-stroke lead over Woods. In a dramatic finish on the final day, Tiger would shoot a 64 in the best final round of his career, but he could not overcome Koepka's hot irons and his 66 score. Koepka's 72-hole total of 264 was 2 shots better than Woods's and set a new PGA Championship record. Koepka took home $1,980,000 for the win. Koepka was the king, but Tiger was back. Watching this play out, St. Louisans and golf fans around the world were once more mesmerized by the sport of golf and St. Louis's turnout and support of the tournament.

Tiger Woods at the 2018 PGA championship
Courtesy of: Getty Images

On the heels of these great showings, the PGA made an announcement that St. Louis will once more host one of golf's greatest matches when the 18th Presidents Cup competition is played at Bellerive Country Club in 2030. The biennial men's team competition pits golfers from the United States against an international squad representing the rest of the world, minus Europe. Once more, golf's finest players and worldwide television audiences will see what a great golf fan base St. Louis has as they will again come to town singing "Meet Me in St. Louie, Louie."

The Day Golf Stopped: 9/11

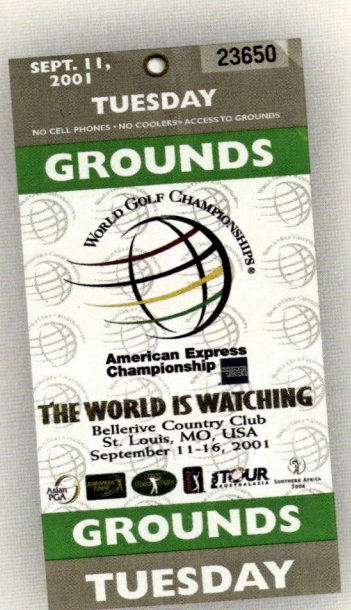

The major golfing event that was supposed to be but never happened was scheduled during one of America's most memorable and horrifying days. Lured by the chance to see Tiger Woods in his first major tournament in St. Louis, thousands of fans were already lining the fairways of Bellerive Country Club to watch the practice rounds under a perfect blue autumn sky. It was September 11, 2001, and they were watching the practice rounds of the American Express Championship sponsored by the World Golf Championship. Woods was playing with Mark Calcavecchia and had already played several holes when word quickly spread that an airplane had crashed into a building in New York. As other golfers continued to stroll out to start their practice rounds or work on their putting, word came of another crash in New York. The buzz amongst the fans and the golfers became more noticeable. Reality soon sank in as everyone began to realize that the two crashes were not just a coincidence but rather terrorism when news arrived of another crash at the Pentagon in Washington, DC.

In the coming hours, everyone realized the world was about to change. The golfing event was cancelled, and all the golfers and fans began thinking about what this tragedy would mean. Many from out of town also had to figure out how to get home. A nationwide ground stop imposed by the FAA immediately shut down all airplane flights for the coming days. The only way to travel during that period would be by car, and Tiger Woods, like many others, drove 17 hours back to Florida.

Tee Shots

There have been many other special moments in the St. Louis region's golf history. The success of the major tournaments elevated St. Louis in golfing circles. St. Louis's major country club courses have hosted dozens of the PGA Tour St. Louis Open, Senior PGA, Senior US Open, and LPGA events on a regular basis since the 1960s. Often sponsored by Johnny Londoff, Michelob Light, or BMW, they have been played at Forest Hills Country Club, Boone Valley, or Fox Run. These events would bring some of the biggest names in the game to town: Annika Sörenstam (4 wins), Kathy Whitworth (3 wins), and Hale Irwin (2 wins), as well as Jack Nicklaus, Arnold Palmer, and Lee Trevino. These events were just big enough to feed the region's hunger for golf's next major event.

Courtesy of: Bill Hudson

Kathy Whitworth in action
Courtesy of: Getty Images

Along the way, St. Louis has developed some of the best golfers on the tour. Belleville's Bob Goalby became the first from the St. Louis region to win a major championship and the only one to bring home a green jacket from Augusta when he won 1968's 32nd edition of the Masters. Goalby had had close finishes in previous years' majors, but this was his best. The final day of play in 1968 should have led to a playoff between Goalby and Argentina's Roberto de Vicenzo. The playoff never happened because de Vicenzo signed his card not realizing that his playing partner Tommy Aaron had put a "4" on the 17th hole when de Vicenzo actually had a birdie "3." The goof was found, a penalty stroke added, and Goalby had a green jacket.

Masters Champion Bob Goalby receives his Green Jacket at Augusta National Golf Club on April 14th, 1968. Courtesy of: Getty Images

Hale Irwin has meant as much to St. Louis golf as anyone. Although he was born in Joplin, he was raised in St. Louis, and he became one of the tour's top golfers from the mid-1970s to the mid-1980s while winning 21 PGA Tour matches. Irwin won three US Opens in 1974, '79, and '90. In the latter win, he became the oldest player to win the championship. He then went on to become one of the leading winners on golf's senior tour.

On the LPGA tour, St. Louis has also had some standout homegrown golfers. Two of the best are Judy Rankin and Ellen Port. As a member of the World Golf Hall of Fame, Judy Rankin may be the best female golfer to come out of the area. From her first win in 1968, Rankin went on to win 26 times on the LPGA tour. Although she never won a majors trophy, she did accomplish four runner-up finishes between 1972 and 1977. Twice, Rankin was selected as the LPGA Player of the Year (1976 and '77). Rankin then went on to become one of golf's leading broadcast commentators.

Ellen Port was a teacher at John Burroughs High School who became one of the nation's best amateur golfers. Port has won the US Women's Mid-Amateur four times and the United

Hale Irwin
Courtesy of: Getty Images

130 | ST. LOUIS SPORTS MEMORIES

States Senior Women's Amateur Golf Championship three times, leaving her tied for the fifth most career wins by a United States Golf Association golfer. She was even a three-time member and one-time captain of America's Curtis Cup team, which takes part in a biennial amateur women's competition between the United States, Great Britain, and Ireland.

There are many other accomplished golfers who called the St. Louis region home, including mother-and-son amateur standouts Barb and Skip Berkmeyer. Barb's biggest wins were claiming five Missouri Women's Amateurs and 10 Missouri State Seniors championships, while Skip's accomplishments made him an 11-time Metropolitan Player of the Year. Belleville's Jay Haas, who also happens to be Bob Goalby's nephew, has had top-five finishes in the Masters (1995), the PGA Championship (1999), and the US Open (1995).

Ellen Port hoists the Curtis Cup trophy
Courtesy of: Getty Images

While the Walker Cup Match has never been played in St. Louis, it does have a very conspicuous tie to the Gateway City. The coveted Walker Cup has been contested every other year since 1922. Initially, it was played on the even years and then switched in the 1940s to be played on the odd years. It pits teams from the United States, Great Britain, and Ireland against one another. The St. Louis connection is in its name. It is named after George Herbert Walker (1875–1953), a wealthy businessman who, at the time of the match's conception, was president of the Unites States Golf Association. Walker was born and grew up in St. Louis. He graduated from Washington University in St. Louis. His grandson (George H. W. Bush) and great-grandson (George W. Bush) both served terms as the President of the United States, and the "W" in their names recognizes their Walker heritage.

Arthur Ashe and Richard Hudlin and the Bennet Historic District

Tennis

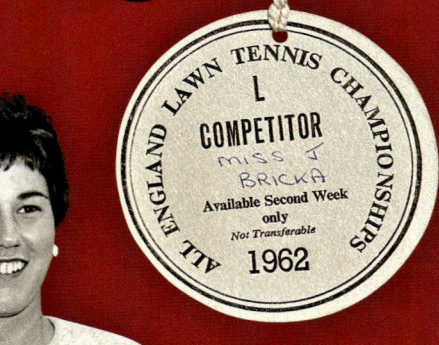

Margaret Smith (left) and Justina Bricka aboard the Queen Elizabeth steamship on their way to compete. Courtesy of: Justina Bricka

Tennis Town

While none of tennis's Majors or Grand Slam tournaments has ever been played in St. Louis, the region's history within the sport is quite strong. One of tennis's most coveted international trophies is named after a St. Louisan. And while pushing the game internationally, he also opened tennis to the masses with hundreds of outdoor courts built throughout the city under his oversight. Another St. Louisan known more for frozen custard than tennis became the first great National Parks champion.

Through the amateur and professional ranks, St. Louisans continued to be a part of tennis history. The names Davis, Buchholz, McKinley, Bricka, Hanks, Eisel, Connors, Ashe, and Flach all had roots in St. Louis while leaving their footprints in the rye grass of Wimbledon or the clay courts of the French and US Opens. The St. Louis Armory, Triple A, and the Dwight Davis Center were all hubs of learning and practicing the game. Coaches Bill Price, Alan Carvel, Richard Hudlin, Larry Miller, and Bill Gatlin all taught and spread tennis.

When his hometown city's segregation policies limited a young African American's development, St. Louis provided him an opportunity to step toward greatness. And then there was the mother-and-grandmother team that instilled and drilled the game into a two-year-old, leading him to one day be the best in the world.

Mary-Ann Eisel
Courtesy of: Getty Images

As tennis's appeal grew in the 1960s, dominant men's and women's players inspired fans on television and in person at center court when the World Tennis League tours came to town. The flame of excitement may have dimmed some lately, but ever since tennis was first played in St. Louis in 1881, its rich and passionate narrative has continued.

Tennis's World Cup

★ ★ ★ ★ ★ ★ ★ ★ ★ ★ ★ ★ ★ ★

The Davis Cup is the premier international men's tennis event. It is the tennis equivalent of soccer's World Cup, and it is named after Dwight Davis, a St. Louisan. Davis was a top tennis player at the turn of the 20th century. He lost in the 1898 finals of the Men's Single US National Championships (later renamed the US Open) but would partner with Holcombe Ward to win three straight men's doubles crowns in the National Championships (1899–1901), also finishing as the runners-up in 1902. A year earlier, in 1901, they were also runners-up at Wimbledon, and three years later Davis would compete in the 1904 Olympics' singles and doubles matches in his own hometown.

The Davis Cup
Courtesy of:
Wikimedia Commons

With the prestige of his tennis career, Davis developed the format and associated trophy for an international Lawn Tennis Challenge that would soon bear his name—the Davis Cup. Besides providing the impetus for this event, Davis captained a team in what was to be the first Davis Cup competition in 1900. He would also play the second time it was held in 1902. Almost 125 years later, the Davis Cup, started by a St. Louisan, remains a prize coveted by all men tennis professionals across the world. The women's equivalent of the Davis Cup is titled the Billie Jean King Cup. Two great players from the ranks of tennis continue to shine upon the annual tennis challenge.

Courtesy of:
Wikimedia Commons

While Davis's cup overflows, as they say, on the international circuit, perhaps his greatest local achievement may be his actions as the St. Louis parks commissioner who expanded the game from tony private clubs to public parks for all to enjoy as he oversaw the construction of hundreds of outdoor courts across the city.

He Really Was Good, Guys and Gals: Ted Drewes

★ ★

His family name brings immediate thoughts of something other than tennis. The Ted Drewes name is synonymous with frozen custard across the St. Louis region, but there was a time in the early 20th century when his tennis prowess exceeded his culinary fame. In fact, when he passed away in 1968, the headlines in the local newspaper referred to him as a "tennis star." It would be six paragraphs before the custard business was mentioned.

Ted Drewes, Sr. began playing tennis in St. Louis at the age of 11 and was soon heralded in newspapers as a teenage tennis phenom. He became a student and protégé of Dwight Davis and went on to win championship titles across the region. His ascendency in the sport began in 1916, when he won the National Muny Recreation Federation title, which was the forerunner of the National Public Parks title. He went on to win the event's singles title in four consecutive years beginning in 1924. Drewes also won the Municipal Tennis Association's singles title 16 times from 1916 to 1936. His name so dominated the Dwight Davis Challenge Trophy between 1914 and 1936 that the trophy was eventually donated to him. Drewes would also win the doubles title 14 times with nine

Ted Drewes, Sr.
Courtesy of: Travis Dillon

Dwight Davis Challenge Trophy
Courtesy of: Travis Dillon

different partners. Ted Drewes, Sr. truly was one of the greatest players developed in St. Louis.

But Drewes was a coach and entrepreneur as well. For 23 years he left his imprint on the game as the tennis coach at Concordia Seminary. He also left St. Louisans with a special treat, his frozen custard stands. How did they come about? During the winters, Ted would go to Florida so he could continue playing tennis year-round. It was in Florida in 1929 that Ted opened his first frozen custard stand to manage while not playing tennis. Returning home in 1930, he opened his first store in St. Louis on Natural Bridge at Goodfellow. A second store would be built on Grand Avenue in 1931 and then another on Chippewa in 1941. Soon Drewes began the tradition of selling Christmas trees stocked from their farm in Nova Scotia.

After a dominant tennis career in the first half of the 20th Century, Ted Drewes' name continues to dominate local media and St. Louis taste buds over a century later.

The Start of a Town's Golden Age

Even with its solid tennis history, St. Louis gained further attention within the world of tennis during the 1960s with an array of stars either coming from or being coached in St. Louis. Many have been inducted into the International Tennis Hall of Fame.

Native St. Louisan Earl Buchholz, Jr. had an outstanding junior tennis career. As an 18-year-old and going by the moniker "Butch," he became an international star as the first to sweep the junior Grand Slam circuit in one playing season. He won the French Open (1958), Wimbledon (1958), the Australian Open (1959), and the US National Boys title (1958). Buchholz had proven himself as the best young player in the world.

Butch Buchholz of the United States returns a shot during a match at the Men's 1965 US Open Tennis Championships. Courtesy of: Getty Images

In 1961, he turned pro and would have many competitive finishes, but he would never win any of tennis's professional Majors or Grand Slam tournaments. Buchholz nevertheless became a driving force in the evolution of the world of professional tennis. In 1968, he was selected to be a part of what was known as the "Handsome Eight," eight men's players signed by the newly formed World Championship Tennis (WCT) group that would play in a series of tournaments around the world. He would win five WCT titles in 1968. In 2005, Buchholz would be inducted into the International Tennis Hall of Fame.

Chuck McKinley holds the trophy after beating Fred Stolle in the final of the Men's Singles, during the Wimbledon Championships July 5, 1963.
Courtesy of: Getty Images

Chuck McKinley would be the region's first Wimbledon winner. He grew up in St. Louis excelling at table tennis before being encouraged to take his game to the big courts. Characterized as being undersized but a dynamo on the court, he took to the game and continued honing his skills in his hometown. McKinley teamed up with Frank Froehling to form one of the nation's best tennis teams at Trinity University in San Antonio, Texas. Interestingly, McKinley would never win an NCAA tennis championship because the tournament overlapped with his play at Wimbledon.

As a college sophomore in 1961, McKinley was a runner-up to Rod Laver in the men's singles final at Wimbledon. The loss was not a setback. He would hoist the winning cups at other championships over the next two years before once more heading into the finals in 1963's Wimbledon singles where he defeated Fred Stolle without ever having lost a set throughout the entire competition.

That same year, McKinley would add two more major championships when he teamed up with John Ralston to win the Davis Cup and the US Men's Doubles Championships. The duo would wind up with two additional US Championships in 1961 and 1964. St. Louis's native son had become the number one player in the world, yet he was not a part of the professional ranks. McKinley continued to play in tournaments as an amateur until the time he retired. He was inducted into the International Tennis Hall of Fame in 1986, which was, unfortunately, the same year he passed away.

Momma Coaches St. Louis's Best: Jimmy Connors

★ ★

Coached by his tennis-playing mother Gloria, Jimmy Connors grew up in East St. Louis before moving to the St. Louis suburb of Belleville on the Illinois side of the Mississippi. Gloria had played for the US National Championship years earlier. She had also once played and defeated the great Babe Didrikson in a match. With that résumé in hand, her career as her son's trainer began when Jimmy was two years old. Coaching alongside Gloria was Jimmy's grandmother Bertha Thompson, an excellent tennis player herself. The lessons and practice would take place almost every day. "Jimbo," as he became known, started a college career that lasted just a single year at UCLA, where he won the NCAA singles title in 1971.

With nothing left to prove in college, Connors turned pro in 1972 and later that year would win his first professional title, the Jacksonville Open. In less than two years, beginning in July 1974, Connors would be ranked the number

Gloria and Jimmy Connors
Courtesy of: Getty Images

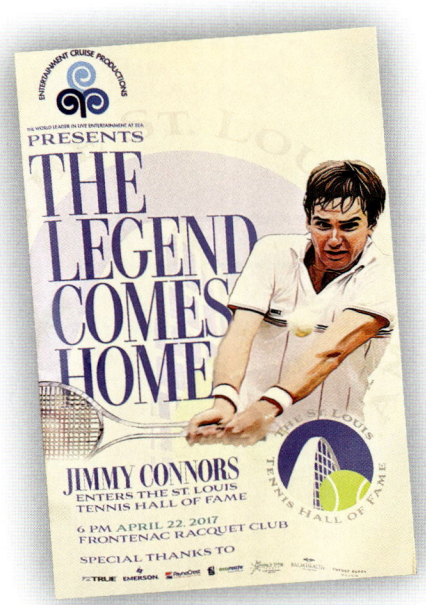

Courtesy of: Terry Ward

one men's tennis player in the world for 160 consecutive weeks. For his career, he would be number one for an amazing 268 weeks—the third-longest reign on the circuit. Connors holds the men's tennis record for most singles titles. Among those 109 wins, Connors would pick up eight Grand Slam Titles: Australian Open (1974), Wimbledon (1974, '82), and US Open (1974, '76, '78, '82, '83).

Connors would also win two Grand Slam doubles titles, partnering with Ilie Nastase at the US Open (1975) and at Wimbledon (1973). When he wasn't winning, he was still making it to the finals. Connors was a runner-up in seven Grand Slam singles finals, one Grand Slam doubles final, and one Grand Slam mixed final.

Connors played with a mental toughness instilled in him from day one by his mother and grandmother, along with a lethal two-handed backhand. With a showman's charisma and a maverick edge, Connors drew fans from all walks. He was inducted into the International Tennis Hall of Fame in 1998, just two years after retiring. Looking back, Momma must have known what she was doing, as her son clearly became one of the world's best to ever play the game.

Champions Made at the Armory

★ ★

Today the St. Louis Armory is being rehabbed into a new apartment, office, and restaurant venue. Located on the south side of Highway 40/64 in midtown St. Louis at 3676 Market Street, the building has played a key role in St. Louis sports over the decades. Built in 1938 for the 128th Infantry Regiment of the Missouri National Guard, the Armory has been more than a building for military drills or a venue for musical acts. It was also used for sports. The football Cardinals would practice there, and the St. Louis Hinder Club (handball) called it their home. More importantly, the St. Louis Armory was the hub of tennis greatness. Many of St. Louis's tennis greats, including Arthur Ashe, Butch Buchholz, and Jimmy Connors, trained and honed their skills at the Armory and credit its slick, varnished floors and its fast bounces for developing their game and greatness.

St. Louis Armory
Courtesy of: Getty Images

In a 2017 interview with *St. Louis Magazine*, Jimmy Connors credited the facility for complementing and enhancing his style of play, an "aggressive, attacking all-out style. The boards were fast, varnished and slick. There was no way to play back; you had to be aggressive and move forward. It was the greatest facility for me. It was the style of play my mom and grandmother were teaching me, and it brought it out more." Rick Randall also described to *St. Louis Magazine* the atmosphere, with "players of all skills hanging out, swapping techniques as they waited for their turn on one of the facility's five courts." The Armory truly made a difference to the players and the world of tennis.

From Richmond to Richmond Heights: Arthur Ashe

From Richmond to Richmond Heights . . . that's the story of Arthur Ashe's rise to become one of tennis's greatest stars. Born and reared in Richmond, Virginia, Arthur Ashe was already becoming an accomplished tennis player before coming to St. Louis in 1960. Ashe's tennis skills had been fine-tuned at Dr. Walter Johnson's tennis camp. Johnson would become his coach and mentor between 1953 and 1960.

Arthur Ashe and Richard Hudlin and the Sumner Tennis Team. Courtesy of: Missouri History Museum, St. Louis

Despite becoming the first African American to play in the Maryland boys' championship (his first integrated tennis competition) in 1958, a change was necessary.

Ashe was a direct decedent of a woman enslaved in North Carolina in 1735. He was growing up in a segregated Richmond, which meant he could not play against white youths or use the city's indoor courts during the colder months of the year. So at the age of 17, Ashe moved to the St. Louis suburb of Richmond Heights to train and live with Richard Hudlin during his senior year at Sumner high school, where he graduated first in his class. The 62-year-old Hudlin was a friend of Dr. Johnson and a teacher and tennis coach at Sumner High School (1930–66). Hudlin had an outstanding tennis résumé. He had played at the University of Chicago and was the team's captain, becoming the first African American team captain in Big Ten tennis. Before Ashe, Hudlin had taken Althea Gibson under his tutelage. She would go on to become the first African American of either gender to compete and then win a Grand Slam with her victory in the French Open in 1956. She would also win at Wimbledon in 1957 and 1958.

In St. Louis, Hudlin was a trailblazer as well. He won a lawsuit in 1945 that would force the Muny Tennis Association to open public tennis facilities to all players regardless of their race. He would go on to become president of the Muny Tennis Association, and it was under his tutelage that Arthur Ashe took the necessary strides to be one of tennis's best.

Not only did the St. Louis Armory's tennis programs under Hudlin allow Ashe to play throughout the year, but its slick and fast hardwood floor made him quicker on the court. There Hudlin converted Ashe from a baseline player to a serve-and-volley specialist. In 1961, Ashe won the previously segregated US Interscholastic Tournament. This was the first of many standout performances from the African American tennis player who for a short time called St. Louis home.

In 1963, Ashe became the first African American selected to the United States Davis Cup team. He received a tennis scholarship to UCLA, where he also graduated first in his class and in 1965 won both the NCAA Singles and Doubles Championships. While winning many professional championships, he won four tennis Grand Slam tournaments: the Australian Open (1970), Wimbledon (1975), the US Open (1968), and the World Championship Tennis Finals (1975). His lone Wimbledon win came against its defending champion and fellow Armory player Jimmy Connors. Ashe's win also marked the first time a male African American player would win tennis' premier event. Ashe would compete in and win four Davis Cup Championships (1963, '68, '69, '70) and was inducted into the International Tennis Hall of Fame in 1985. His was a storied career that may never have happened if it had not been for an elder tennis coach and the integrated policies of St. Louis.

Doubles Was His Game, Flach Was His Name

★ ★

St. Louisan Ken Flach was a tennis doubles machine during the 1980s. He grew up and found his tennis game in suburban Kirkwood before heading across the Mississippi to play for Southern Illinois University at Edwardsville. SIUE had just come off two NCAA Division II men's doubles championships led by Juan Farrow in 1979 and 1980. The torch soon passed to Flach when he won the NCAA Division II (DII) men's singles championships in 1981, '82, and '83. Flach lost the DII doubles title match in 1981, but won it in 1982 and '83, playing with a different partner each year. It was in the 1983 doubles win that Flach found a partner from Minnesota in Robert Seguso, sending both men down the path to international tennis fame.

Flach and Seguso would dominate the men's doubles circuit. They would win Wimbledon in 1987 and '88 and the US Open in 1985 (runners-up in 1987 and '89). As doubles partners in the 1988 Olympics in Seoul, the two brought home the gold medal. Flach would go on to win one more US Open Doubles Championship in 1993 with a new partner, Rich Leach. Leach's career included four Grand Slam doubles and four mixed doubles titles.

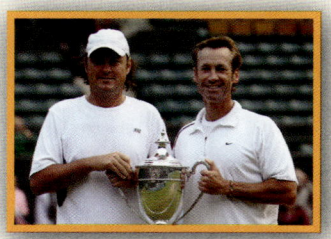

Robert Seguso and Ken Flach (right) celebrate winning at Wimbledon in 2008.
Courtesy of: Getty Images

Flach was also a two-time Grand Slam mixed doubles champion, winning the 1986 Wimbledon and French Open titles with Kathy Jordan, herself a winner of seven Grand Slam titles.

Six Grand Slam tournament wins and an Olympic gold medal definitely qualify St. Louis–reared Ken Flach as one of tennis's greatest doubles players of all time.

The Golden Girls

When fans think of great St. Louis tennis players, they think of the four men who won a combined 18 Grand Slams. But this raises the question of whether there were any great women tennis players from St. Louis. The answer is a definitive yes. While St. Louis women have played in many Grand Slam tournaments, only one has brought home a winner. That does not dilute their importance and contributions to the game. St. Louis has produced three of the country's top 10 players of their era in Justina Bricka, Carol Hanks, and Mary-Ann Eisel. Not only were the three all reared in St. Louis, but they would all soon become partners on the court internationally.

St. Louis's Best, from top left clockwise: Carol Hanks, Justina Bricka, and Mary-Ann Eisel.
Courtesy of: Justina Bricka

Justina Bricka's ranking certificate
Courtesy of: Justina Bricka

University City High School star Justina Bricka was a regular in the singles, doubles, and mixed doubles Grand Slam tournaments between 1959 and 1965. She was nationally ranked among the top 10 players in 1961, 1962, and 1964. Her best finish was in 1962, when she partnered with that year's top-ranked women's tennis player, Margaret Smith

FORGOTTEN TEAMS AND MOMENTS FROM AMERICA'S BEST SPORTS TOWN | 145

Justina Bricka's Wimbeldon Medal–1962
Courtesy of: Justina Bricka

of Australia. The duo reached the finals of the French Open but were relegated to runners-up by the South African team of Sandra Price and Renee Schuurman. Twice, Justina and her partner would reach the semifinals at Wimbledon (1962 doubles and 1964 mixed doubles). She would also reach the semifinals of the 1964 US Open playing with fellow St. Louisan Carol Hanks. In 1961, Justina helped the US team win the Wightman Cup by beating that year's Wimbledon winner, Angela Mortimer. The Wightman Cup was an annual women's team tennis competition contested between the United States and Great Britain from 1923 through 1989.

Over a five-year span between 1960 and 1964, Carol Hanks (married name Aucamp) would be ranked as one of the top 12 women's players in the United States. She too was a regular on the Grand Slam tennis tour in the early 1960s. In 1966, Hanks had her best Grand Slam finish when she and her partner, Ed Rubinoff, were runners-up in the US National Cup (US Open) mixed doubles tournament. Her winning ways began at John Burroughs High School before she headed off to Stanford University, where she won the US Indoor doubles championship partnering with Linda Yeomans in 1962. Her singles résumé includes the Cincinnati title in 1960, the US Hardcourt title in 1962, and the US Indoor title in 1963.

Justina Bricka's Wightman Cup
Courtesy of: Justina Bricka

In doubles play, Hanks often teamed up with fellow St. Louisans for wins. In 1960, she partnered with Justina Bricka to win the Cincinnati title. In 1961, she and Justina defeated Billie Jean King and Karen Susman to win the National Clay Court Championship. That same year the twosome became the first two St. Louis women to compete at Wimbledon, where they lost in the first round. Hanks won the US

Indoor Doubles title in 1958, '63, '64, and '65. St. Louisan Mary-Ann Eisel was her partner in the latter three wins. In 1963, when Hanks and her partner Arthur Ashe played in Wimbledon's mixed doubles competition, they become the tournament's first interracial team to win a match there. They lost in the quarterfinals. Hanks and Bricka teamed up once more and made it to the semifinals of the 1964 US Open.

Carol Hanks Aucamp
Courtesy of: Carol Hanks Aucamp

Hanks's frequent partner and Ladue High School graduate, Mary-Ann Eisel (married name Beattie), was also a regular in Grand Slam competitions during this period and reached the finals twice. She would play at Wimbledon nine times. Between 1964 and 1971, Eisel would regularly be ranked within the top 10 women players. In 1964, she teamed up with Justina Bricka to win the Irish National Doubles title. In 1967, she partnered with Donna Floyd only to lose to Rosemary Casals and Billie Jean King in the US Championship's women's finals. A year later she partnered with her future and former husband, Britain's Peter Curtis, to win the US Open Mixed Doubles Championship and become the only St. Louis woman to date with a Grand Slam win.

These three women would continue playing and winning on the tennis circuit for another decade, and they would remain an inspiration to all the young girls playing on tennis courts across the St. Louis region.

Aces & Slims

★ ★

Across all of the major sports, there is a history of teams only playing one or two seasons. Within St. Louis's sports history, it has had its share of one-year wonders. The 1985 St. Louis Slims were one such team. The Slims were one of eight teams that played in the Domino's Pizza Team Tennis League (a.k.a. World Team Tennis) that year.

Each team in the league had two male and two female players from the pro tour. Interestingly, the players received no salary. Their earnings came from an incentive package based on wins. The total prize purse for the league was only $400,000, which didn't entice any of tennis's major players to join the league. Like the other teams, St. Louis players were journeyman names: Sandy Collins, John Mattke, Terry Moor, and Candy Reynolds. The Slim's tenure was quite short—just 14 matches (nine wins and five losses) between July 10 and August 13. The matches were simple five-set affairs, with a men's and then women's match followed by a men's and women's doubles match, and then a Mixed doubles set.

The team was owned by the owner of the St. Louis Blues, Harry Ornest, who also owned the Arena, where the team played. Although the

148 | ST. LOUIS SPORTS MEMORIES

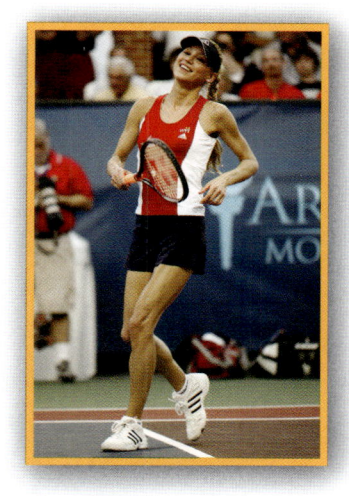

Anna Kournikova
Courtesy of: Getty Images

Slims would lose in the postseason finals, Ornest could not have been happy with a season high attendance of just 700.

Tenure-wise, the Aces lasted much longer. They entered the World Team Tennis League (WTT) in 1994 and would play 18 seasons until the WTT folded in 2011. During that time, they won only won one WTT Championship. In 1996, they beat the Delaware Smash for the top spot in the eight-team league. Over the years, the WWT matches spurred interest in tennis by bringing many famous players like Lindsey Davenport, Anna Kournikova, John McEnroe, Andy Roddick, and Pete Sampras, as well as Serena and Venus Williams, to the Aces' home court at the Dwight Davis Memorial Tennis Center in Forest Park. The tennis-loving Apted family (of Miss Hullings and the Cheshire Inn fame) had bought the team in 2005 from the Dwight Davis Memorial Tennis Center. Even though the Aces folded, the Apted family continued their love and support of tennis through their Creve Coeur Racquet Club. Like the St. Louis Browns, the Aces lost more games than they won, yet they brought the excitement of the game and many of its greatest players to the Gateway City.

St. Louis Aces Franchise Record

YEAR	WINS	LOSSES	PCT.
1994	2	12	0.143
1995	7	9	0.438
1996	11	2	0.846
1997	8	6	0.571
1998	6	8	0.429
1999	3	9	0.250
2000	4	10	0.286
2001	8	6	0.571
2002	4	10	0.286
2003	4	10	0.286
2004	6	8	0.429
2005	9	5	0.643
2006	8	6	0.571
2007	9	5	0.643
2008	3	11	0.214
2009	5	9	0.357
2010	7	7	0.500
2011	8	6	0.571
TOTAL	112	139	0.446

Racing

They're Off and Running!

★ ★

While the St. Louis region may not host anything like horse racing's Triple Crown, it does have a lengthy history of fans regularly gathering to watch the horses race. Interestingly, that history has taken place on the east side of the Mississippi River at two racetracks: Cahokia Downs and Fairmont Park.

Fairmont Park, in Collinsville, Illinois, has the longer history of the two tracks. It opened in 1925 and has featured both thoroughbred flat racing and Standardbred harness racing, although the latter was discontinued in 1999. The track began hosting the very popular Fairmont Derby back in the 1920s and today still hosts regularly scheduled races throughout the week during the racing season.

The East Saint Louis Jockey Club began offering horse racing at Cahokia Downs in Alorton, Illinois, in 1954. For many years it was a special stop for St. Louisans to see Standardbred harness racing and Thoroughbred flat racing events throughout the racing season until it completely shut down in 1980. A historic event happened at Cahokia Downs on October 18, 1978, when jockey David Gall became the first rider in US Thoroughbred horse racing to win eight races on a single race card.

Gall was a regular at both Cahokia Downs and Fairmont tracks, and with his impressive résumé was the one locals would likely bet on. Gall was the winner of the US National Riding title in recognition of his having won more races than any other rider in 1979 and 1981. When he retired, he ranked fifth in lifetime wins by a North American jockey with 7,394 victories.

David Gall
Courtesy of:
St. Louis Sports Hall of Fame

FORGOTTEN TEAMS AND MOMENTS FROM AMERICA'S BEST SPORTS TOWN

Horses Weren't All That Raced: Auto Racing

★ ★

As society transitioned from horses to cars, it was only natural that the sport of racing would as well. While initially never big on the circuit, St. Louis has had its moments, along with a few bumps in the road. Auto racing's popularity took root from the 1950s to the 1970s, when there were fewer forms of entertainment. Heading to the racetrack offered action and excitement. Flashing back to the mid-1960s, there was a distinct commercial that could be heard on radio stations like KXOK or KIRL filled with the rush and roar of the announcer shouting over the background noise of racing engines about an upcoming racing event and telling listeners to, "Be There! This Saturday! M–A–R, Mid-America Raceway for the . . ."

Built in 1965 and located near Wentzville (a St. Louis suburb), Mid-America Raceway was a 1200-foot dragstrip along with a 2.89 mile road course that gave St. Louisans a venue to feed their hunger for local auto racing. In spring of 1966, MAR followed Sebring as the host of the second Sports Car Club of America's (SCCA) Trans Am race. It also became a site for car, truck, and motorcycle races. Over the years, the raceway would host many drag and road races. St. Louis's National and Regional races were held there until 1984, when Wayne Meinert's St. Louis International Raceway opened in East St. Louis and MAR closed.

While academy award–winning actor Paul Newman's love of racing was well known, fewer people are aware that on numerous occasions, he was a winner of national championships as a driver in the SCCA and could often be found racing at Mid-America Raceways.

There were many other raceways spread across the area during this period, from Lake Hill Speedway in Valley Park to the Belleclair track in Belleville. Granite City's Tri-City Speedway was a popular destination with its high-banked 3/8-mile oval dirt racetrack. Tri-City still offers racing fans an opportunity to enjoy their sport, but the growing interest in the sport is now fed by the expanded racing complex built by Meinert.

Wayne Meinert had initially constructed a 1/8-mile drag strip on what was once river bottom land on the east side of the Mississippi River back in 1967. Initially called St. Louis Raceway Park, the track was expanded to a 1/4-mile track three years later and rebranded as St. Louis International Raceway. Racing became the name of the game over the next decade, with many different racing series coming to Meinert's facility. By 1985, a 2.6-mile road course was added along with a new name, Gateway International Raceway. Others simply referred to it as "The Swamp" due to the damp climate of the river bottoms area. For the next two decades the course would continue to satisfy race fans with a racing schedule, but nothing from the ranks of big-name racing held elsewhere on the circuit. In 1995, that would change.

Long Beach Grand Prix promoter Chris Pook purchased Gateway in 1995. His vision was to bring IndyCar and NASCAR races to his newly acquired track. To do so meant a rebuild of the facility. A new speedway oval with an infield road course was constructed with an NHRA (National Hot Rod Association) sanctioned drag strip built alongside.

The new facility was christened in May 1997 with a CART (Championship Auto Racing Teams) race. In the ensuing months, the NHRA and NASCAR circuits also held events, and the St. Louis region seemed to have become a hot commodity in racing circles. There was an eventual switch from the CART to IndyCar series as well as a program expansion to include Truck Series events at Gateway. Things seemed to be going well for St. Louis racing. In 2010, Pook sold the facility to Dover Motorsports Inc. The new ownership hosted two Nationwide Series but was shocked by the disappointing fan turnout and the impact of the financial crisis of the previous years. Without the fans and revenue, they ceased operations at Gateway before the end of 2010.

A year later, Curtis Francois, a retired racecar driver and real estate developer, purchased the property with the goal of offering a 2012 racing season. He laid out a formidable and diverse racing schedule with an emphasis on drag racing and once more changed the course's name to Gateway Motorsports Park. Under his leadership, the property became a premiere racing venue in IndyCar, NASCAR, and NHRA racing. In 2019, World Wide Technology acquired the naming rights for the track, which is now called World Wide Technology Raceway at Gateway. The track has since hosted the Bommarito Automotive Group 500 and the NTT IndyCar Series and successfully hosted the sold-out inaugural NASCAR Cup series, titled the "Enjoy Illinois 300," in June 2022 that is destined to become a regular stop on the NASCAR circuit for a long time.

Alex Peroni (5) Carlin Racing drives through turn three during the testing for the Indy Lights Series on August 19, 2021, at World Wide Technology Raceway at Gateway in Madison, Illinois. Courtesy of: Getty Images

Chess

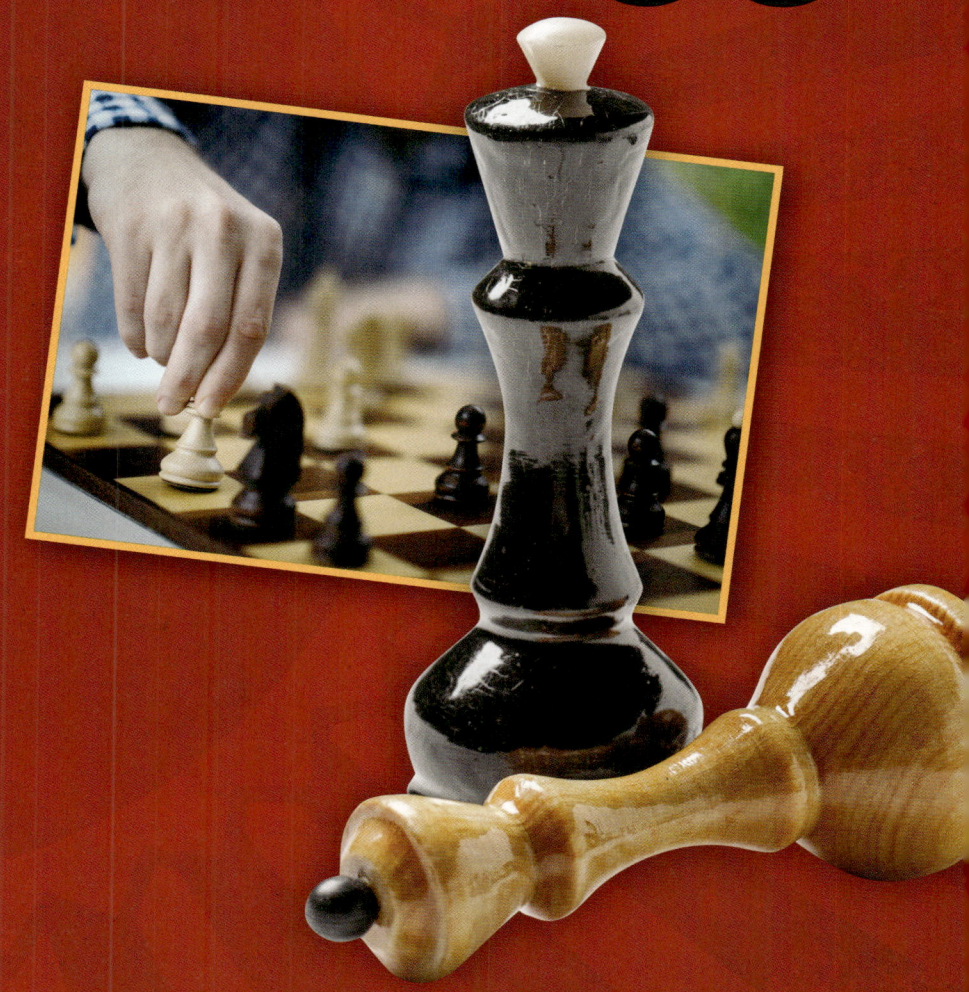

Chess Is a Sport, and St. Louis Is Its Capital

While some readers might not think of chess as a sport, the International Olympic Committee (IOC) recognizes it as such, as do more than 100 countries around the world. The IOC's recognition is an acknowledgment of the sport-like aspects of the game. The same national fervor that can be found in the Olympic Games, be it basketball, hockey, or gymnastics, can also be found in the sport of chess and its worldwide matches.

Saint Louis Chess Club co-founder Rex Sinquefield playing chess outside of the Saint Louis Chess Club. Courtesy of: Saint Louis Chess Club, Lennart Ootes

The support of Rex Sinquefield (the St. Louis native who is often called the greatest chess sponsor in American history), through the establishment of the Saint Louis Chess Club and the World Chess Hall of Fame, has led to recognition of the Gateway City as the premiere chess destination worldwide. Chess Master Jeff Kastner notes that Sinquefield's efforts over the last two decades helped St. Louis surpass New York City as a chess mecca. In recognition of these accomplishments, the United States Congress in 2014 designated St. Louis as the Chess Capital of the United States. Since then, the honor has been extended worldwide.

Historians believe chess likely started over a thousand years ago in India and has evolved across cultures and history into the game played today. St. Louis first stepped into the chess limelight back in 1886, when the city hosted segments of the first World Chess Championship.

The city once again took center stage when it hosted the seventh annual Chess Congress alongside the 1904 World's Fair. The city's fascination continued into the 1940s and through the 1970s, when Missouri's premiere chess talent and regular district champion Robert Steinmeyer drew many Grandmasters of the game to town to challenge him.

A renaissance of the sport was taking place in mid-America at the turn of the 21st Century as the Saint Louis Chess Club was founded in 2007 and opened its doors a year later. In 2009, just across the street from the Chess Club in the city's Central West End, the World Chess Hall of Fame was established. Through Sinquefield's efforts, the Chess Club and Scholastic Centre of St. Louis became, according to *Esquire* magazine, "the headquarters of American Chess." The 6,000 square foot Centre was not set up simply to preserve and provide education on the history of the game; it is a facility to honor and host the sport. The complex includes a hall for tournaments, classrooms, a library, and a play area. It hosts thousands of members of all skill levels, from beginners to World Champions.

As a footnote to the city's chess grandeur and an addition to its many other sports national championships, Saint Louis University grabbed another title by winning the President's Cup for the Collegiate Chess National Championship on April 3, 2022. Members of Coach Alejandro Ramirez's team

The 9th Sinquefield Cup was played from August 16th to 28th, 2021–French Grandmaster Maxime Vachier-Lagrave (Left) with Rex Sinquefield. Courtesy of: Saint Louis Chess Club, Lennart Ootes

were Cemil Can Ali Marandi, Dariusz Swiercz, Nikolas Thodorou, Akshat Chandra, Benjamin Bok, and Robby Kevlishvilli. The exuberant coach declared that "Now SLU is undoubtedly the number one chess university in the country," and the team's hometown is the number one chess city in the world!

Professional Wrestling

JOE GARAGIOLA
AND
WRESTLING at the CHASE
9 to 10 P.M.
Every Saturday Night
Matching such great wrestlers as
Gorgeous George, The Mighty Atlas,
Whipper Billy Watson, Rip Hawk.

Channel **11** KPLR-TV

Wrestling at the
1904 Olympics
Courtesy of: Missouri History Museum, St. Louis

Wrestling moved
to the KPLR-TV Studio
Courtesy of: Mercantile Library

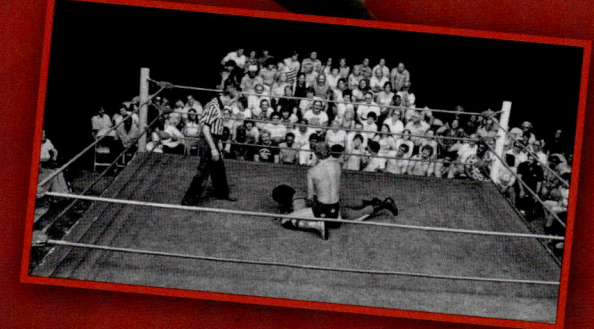

Rasslin's Capital

★★★★★★★★★★★★★★★★★★★★

St. Louis has always been a hub for professional wrestling. The city played a key role in the transformation of wrestling away from the Greco-Roman form of the sport that dates back to those ancient cultures. During the 1904 Olympic Games held in St Louis in conjunction with that year's World's Fair, freestyle wrestling was first introduced at the games. It brought a new dimension of moves and action that would soon displace the staid and simplistic methods of the Greco-Roman style.

As vaudeville entertainment soon swept across America in the 1920s, professional wrestling began taking on aspects of showmanship. It became more of a pseudo-sport or simply "theatre on a mat" as wrestlers quenched Americans' thirst for entertainment with action and hyperbole during a time when there were no televisions or video games.

For over four decades, one St. Louisan was front and center in the evolution of professional wrestling, or "rasslin" as many would call it. His name was Sam Muchnick, the son of Ukrainian immigrant parents who settled in the Gateway City. Muchnick's career began as a newspaper columnist covering the St. Louis Cardinals in the

Sam Muchnick (right) watches wrestler Buddy Rodgers sign his contract
Courtesy of: Katie Muchnick Schneider

1920s and 1930s. He would also cover boxing and wrestling. The latter soon led him to join Tom Packs Promotions in bringing those two sports to St. Louis fans. After some disagreements with Packs, Muchnick began his own promotions, a move that would eventually lead to St. Louis becoming the professional wrestling capital of the world. A major part of the city's prominence was one very special television program.

Kiel Auditorium Wrestling sellout
Courtesy of: Missouri History Museum, St. Louis

Muchnick became one of the most prominent men in the sport. Between 1950 and 1983 he became the leader of the newly formed National Wrestling Alliance, and he did it all out of St. Louis. Over the next three decades, St. Louis was the place to be during the sport's golden years, thanks in large part to Muchnick. Wrestler Ric Flair summed up the feelings of his contemporaries when he said: "In the year 1978, Terry Funk told me if I wanted to be a star in this business, I had to get to St. Louis on Friday Night. You know what I'm talking about. I had to be at the Kiel or the Arena, I had to be live at the Chase, I had to be in St. Louis if I wanted to be a star."

Once or twice a month, tens of thousands of wrestling fans would pack Kiel Auditorium or the St. Louis Arena to watch and cheer on their heroes: Gorgeous George, Lou Thesz, Pat O'Connor, Dick the Bruiser, Jack Briscoe, Cowboy Bob Ellis, King Kong Brody, and others. But 1958 also saw the birth of one of the most remembered spectacles of the sport: *Wrestling at the Chase*. The iconic television program, which ran for 24 years, came together in a conversation on an airplane ride between Sam Muchnick and Harold Koplar, the owner of both the Chase Park Plaza Hotel and the soon-to-be KPLR television station. Muchnick was looking to enhance his wrestling enterprise, and Koplar was looking for television programing. What the two men put together was one of the most memorable television programs of all time. How memorable and popular was it? Only the local news and Cardinals baseball had higher viewership.

The program first aired on May 23, 1959, when most St. Louisans were lucky to have even one television per household and homes weren't as big as they are today. People didn't have a living room and a family room. They had a front room with a television set that at the time had only three channels providing programing. The whole family would be huddled around the lone television day in and day out seeking entertainment. When KPLR-TV arrived to add a fourth station to all-day viewing, it brought with it this new show that people instantly fell in love with and subsequently provided memories of a lifetime.

While most matches on the wrestling circuit were happening in dark and dank VFW halls or arenas, Wrestling at the Chase offered something different. It brought wrestling into the most opulent setting in St. Louis, the Chase Park Plaza Hotel. As the advertising slogans noted, "the Chase was the Place." It was the place where anyone who was anybody stayed, from presidents to royalty to movie stars. It was where the likes of Frank Sinatra, Dean Martin, Nat King Cole, and America's other stars performed—and now there would be wrestling. Wrestling became the hottest ticket in town. People came to watch and be watched ringside dressed to the nines, while tens of thousands of wrestling fans watched the matches on television in their homes each Saturday night or with the re-airing of the program on Sunday morning. In a simpler time with fewer entertainment options, fans ringside or at home loved wrestling, real or not. These decades of St. Louis's ascendancy to the top of the wrestling world ended with the historic growth of Vince McMahon's World Wrestling Entertainment (WWE) after Sam Muchnick's retirement in 1983. But WWE may never have been possible had it not been for Sam Muchnick and St. Louis's support for professional wrestling.

Early Wrestling in the Khorassan Room
Courtesy of: Katie Muchnick Schneider

Boxing

September 25, 1962, Comiskey Park, Chicago, IL—Sonny Liston watches as Floyd Patterson falls to the canvas after being hit by a hard left hook in the first round of their championship fight. Courtesy of: Getty Images

Michael Spinks
Courtesy of:
Wikimedia Commons

Knockouts

★ ★

Even with all the athleticism involved in professional wrestling, it remains simply "theatre on a mat" played out for entertainment. Professional boxing, on the other hand, while also entertainment, remains as real as a punch to the mouth. Across boxing's long history, multiple St. Louisans have worn championship belts. Henry Armstrong, Sonny Liston, and Leon and Michael Spinks are the most prominent.

While he fought nearly a century ago, Henry Armstrong, a product of Vashon High School, at 5' 6" and fighting at between 124 and 146 pounds, remains today the only boxer to hold three world titles at the same time. In 1938, he was the reigning featherweight,

Henry Armstrong
Courtesy of:
Wikimedia Commons

lightweight, and welterweight champion of the world. Interestingly, jazz singer Al Jolson and Hollywood heavy George Raft were part of the team that managed Armstrong. Many within the fight game still consider him, pound for pound, the greatest fighter in boxing history. In 1937 alone, he was 27-0, winning 26 of the bouts by knockouts. His career record was 151-21 with 101 knockouts, with winnings of more than $1 million.

When thinking of Sonny Liston, the picture that quickly comes to mind is that of Liston lying on the mat with vociferous underdog Cassius Clay (Muhammad Ali) taunting him from above in their 1965 heavyweight rematch. Liston had come to St. Louis as a teenager but soon fell into a life of crime. His tenure in Missouri's state prison changed things and turned Liston's life around. There he learned the art of boxing and took up the sport full time upon his release. His prowess within Golden Glove matches led to a dominating professional career and rise to the rank of number one contender. However, he was originally denied a chance to fight for the title because of his criminal past and alleged ties to organized crime. Despite pleas not to fight Liston from the NAACP and even President Kennedy, reigning heavyweight champion Floyd Patterson conceded to a title match at Chicago's Comiskey Park in 1962. The fight didn't last long, as Liston knocked out the champ at 2:06 in the first round. A rematch a year later confirmed Liston as the true champion as he once again KO'ed Patterson, this time at 2:10 in the first round.

Next up for Liston was the brash young Cassius Clay, the Olympic gold-medal heavyweight winner who was taking the boxing world by storm. The two met for a title match in February 1964. It ended in a draw due to an injury to Liston's shoulder after the 6th round. Once Liston healed, a title rematch took place in May 1965. In a controversial set of circumstances that still are debated today, Clay put Liston down in less than 2 minutes in the first round. The exact time and events remain in debate, but in any event Liston was down and Clay was still

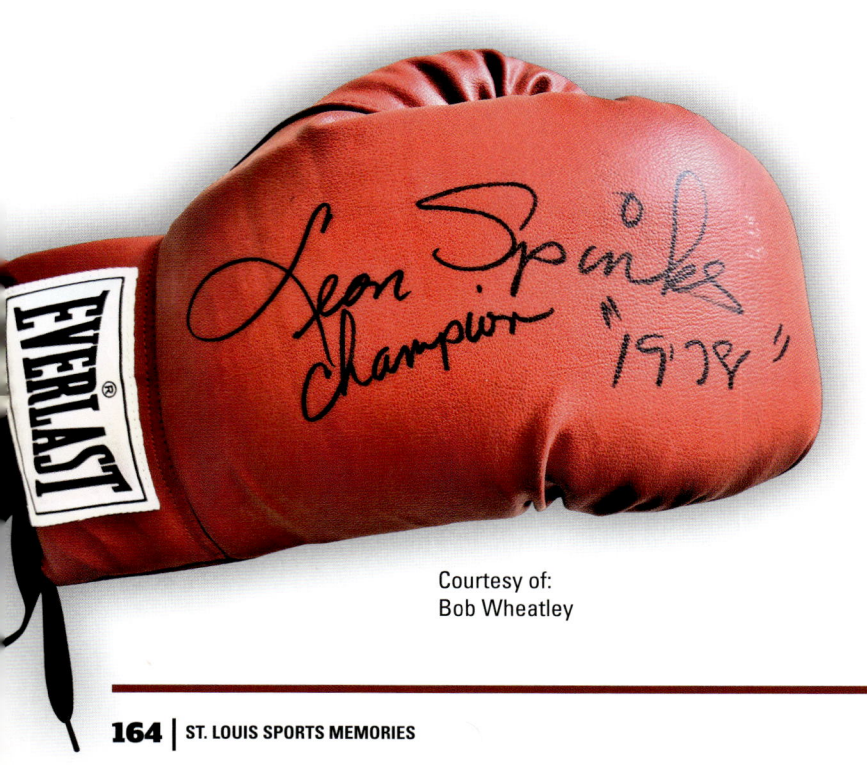

Courtesy of:
Bob Wheatley

standing, becoming the new champ while also declaring himself "the greatest." Liston continued to fight until 1970 while living in the shadows of his past, but two things are still undeniable. He once was the Heavyweight Champion of the World with a career record of 50-4 (39 KOs), and he was reared in St. Louis.

Two brothers growing up in the St. Louis housing projects boxed their way to the Olympics and then to the top of their sport. Leon and Michael Spinks each won gold medals in the 1976 Montreal games. They would become the only pair of brothers to hold world heavyweight titles until Ukrainian boxers Vitali and Wladimir Klitschko attained the same feat decades later. Leon, the older of the two, would score first with one of boxing's biggest upsets in February 1978. He beat Muhammad Ali in a 15-round split decision. It was only his eighth pro fight. The championship was short-lived. Spinks would lose in a title rematch in September of that year. He would fight another 37 times but never again as a champion before retiring in 1990 with a record of 26-17-3 (14 KOs). His son Cory would follow his father to a championship by winning the welterweight title in 2003.

Michael had won the middleweight gold in the 1976 Olympics. Turning pro a year later, Michael would capture the light heavyweight title from Eddie Mustafa Muhammad in 1981. After defending his title several times, Spinks challenged heavyweight champion Larry Holmes, whose 48-0 record was one shy of boxing legend Rocky Marciano's 49-0 mark. Holmes never tied it. Spinks beat him in a 15-round unanimous decision to become boxing's first-ever world light-heavyweight champion to win the world heavyweight championship. He would win a rematch with Holmes the next year and win two more matches before being KO'd in the first round by Mike Tyson in June 1988. That would be his last match. He had had enough and retired with a 31-1 record consisting of 21 knockouts.

The Best Ever

Jackie Joyner-Kersee
Courtesy of: Getty Images

Jackie Joyner-Kersee

★★★★★★★★★★★★★★★★★★★★★★★

The St. Louis region has produced many great athletes, all with very special skills and athleticism. Many have even risen to the top of their sport. Yet there may be one absolutely pure athlete who truly is the "best of the best."

Born in East St. Louis, Illinois, in 1962 and named after then first lady Jaqueline Kennedy, she became the region's international superstar. Her name is Jackie Joyner-Kersee. As a five-time Olympian, she won three gold, one silver, and two bronze medals performing in the heptathlon and long jump. The heptathlon consists of seven events (100-meter hurdles, high jump, shot put, 200-meter dash, long jump, javelin, and 800-meter run). She won the event in the Olympics twice and finished second another time. Between 1986 and 1998, Joyner would win nine gold medals in the World Championships, Goodwill Games, and Pan American Games. All of that was on top of a college career that included playing basketball at UCLA. How superior was Joyner-Kersee in her performances? Today she still holds the heptathlon world record and the next six all-time best results as well as the second-best distance in the long jump.

It is no wonder that in 1987, even before she completed her career, Sports Illustrated named her the Greatest Female Athlete of the 20th Century. The awards are so numerous it is hard to list them all, but in 2001, she was also selected as the "Top Woman Collegiate Athlete of the Last 25 Years." Jackie Joyner-Kersee's accomplishments stand out even in the star-studded field of St. Louis athletes.

The Announcers

Joe, Harry, and Jack called Cardinal baseball.
Courtesy of:
St. Louis Media Museum

They Made Us Love the Game

★ ★

St. Louis's recognition as a sports leader is due to its supportive and knowledgeable fan base. St. Louisans love their teams and regularly lead the various sports in attendance—even when some of those teams do not play so well. This love and knowledge of the games is nurtured and encouraged by the men and women with a special talent for bringing the games to the people. They do it on the radio, on television, and in print. It is their calling and writing that has made St. Louis fans the best, and they too have been recognized as the best in the business.

In the days when there was only radio, these announcers painted the picture of the game for the fans with their words and delivery. You saw the action in your head, perhaps while listening on your transistor radio. It was like being there in the stadium watching when you would hear Harry Caray begin his description of almost every pitch with ". . . the pitcher toes the rubber, looks in, gets the sign . . . here's the wind up, the stretch, the pitch." In some situations, Caray would then exclaim "there she goes, way back, it might be, it could be, it is—a home run!" There are just so many memorable calls that we hold on to in order to relive our teams' rich history. Who can forget Jack Buck's famous, "go crazy folks, go crazy!" on Ozzie Smith's playoff homer or Mike Shannon's "get up baby, get up."

Yes, the Gateway City was blessed with many great sports announcers, going back to baseball's France Laux, Johnny O'Hara, and Dizzy Dean. Then came Harry Caray, Buddy Blattner, Joe Garagiola, Jack Buck, Mike Shannon, John Rooney, Tim McCarver, and Dan McLaughlin. Joe Buck even got his start in St. Louis sitting next to his dad calling games. Caray, Jack Buck, Garagiola, and McCarver are all headlined in

Cooperstown as recipients of broadcasting's Ford Frick Award for their contributions to the game.

The highly acclaimed Bob Costas came to St. Louis to start his career calling Spirits basketball and educated St. Louisans on sports as he hosted KMOX's *Sports Open Line* show. He then added baseball, the Olympics, and almost every other sport, as well as also becoming a Ford Frick Award winner.

When thinking about hockey's top announcers, St. Louis likely had the best in Dan Kelly. The winner of the Foster Hewitt Memorial Award for excellence in ice hockey broadcasting, Kelly brought Blues hockey into St. Louis households for 21 seasons before succumbing to cancer at too early an age. Not only did he leave his famous "HE SHOOTS, HE SCORRRES!" call for all of us to remember, he also left his sons Dan and John to carry on in their father's footsteps in the booth.

Hockey's Best–Dan Kelly
Courtesy of: St. Louis Media Museum

And in America's soccer town, how lucky are St. Louis fans to have one of the game's best in Bill McDermott? He has spent over 45 years announcing all levels of the game, from local sports to NCAA tournaments to Major League Soccer matches, and even the World Cup. Since his early days covering the Stars, he has earned the title "Mr. Soccer."

In print, St. Louis has had some of the best sportswriters of all time to keep fans informed about their sports. Four have been selected for the Baseball Writers Association of America award as recognized by Baseball's Hall of Fame. These special men are J. G. Taylor Spink (1962), J. Roy Stockton (1972), Bob Broeg (1979), and Rick Hummel (2006). Although not recognized for the award, but known as "The Benchwarmer," Bob Burnes was the longtime outstanding sportswriter for the *St. Louis Globe-Democrat*. These are the standouts who taught us sports. They painted the games' pictures in our minds, and those images remain today as our very own sports memories.

We Cheered There

Sportsman's Park Aerial View
Courtesy of: St. Louis Browns
Historical Society & Fan Club

Sportsman's Park

★ ★

While many think of Sportsman's Park as a baseball park, it was a venue for many different sports and events over the century that it sat at the hustling and bustling corner of Grand and Dodier on St. Louis's north side. The park's address was 2911 Grand Avenue, and it was bordered by Grand Avenue on the east, Dodier Street on the south, Spring Avenue on the west, and Sullivan Avenue on the north. When the Cardinals moved into the stadium, they used an office address of 3623 Dodier Street.

The first baseball games known to be played on the site took place in 1867. At that time, it was known as the Grand Avenue Ball Grounds and would be renamed as Sportsman's Park in 1876. It would become the home of St. Louis's first National League team, the St. Louis Brown Stockings. The first grandstands weren't built until 1881, four years after the Brown Stockings were removed from the league. It would remain the home of another Brown Stockings team as they began their rise in the American Association, but it would not be their home field when they joined the National League in 1892. The team instead moved to a new field a few blocks away that would be called Robison Field. When the American League Browns moved to St. Louis in 1902, they took up ownership of the field until they departed in 1953, when the Cardinals then took possession. The Cardinals had actually been playing in Sportsman's Park since 1920, when they moved in as tenants after a fire destroyed their

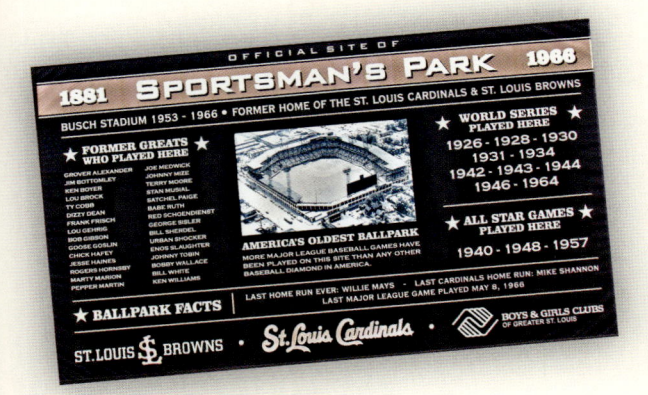

172 | ST. LOUIS SPORTS MEMORIES

field—the last wooden grandstand in the majors. With both the Browns and Cardinals playing in the same stadium all those years, Sportsman's Park became the leader in most games played in a professional ballpark. The stadium would play host to ten World Series (1926, '28, '30, '31, '34, '42, '43, '44, '46, and '64) and three All-Star games (1940, '48, and '57).

As a harbinger of the times, on May 24, 1940, the Browns played their first night game under newly installed lights. The Cardinals would get their first night game a few weeks later on June 4th. On May 5, 1944, Sportsman's Park was the last Major League ballpark to end its policy of restricting African Americans to the bleachers and the right-field pavilion. Leading up to that milestone, The Kansas City Monarchs and Chicago American Giants were scheduled to play a special July 4th Negro League game in 1941. Monarch Star Satchel Paige demanded that the stadium be open and integrated or he wouldn't play. Paige's demands were met, and a sellout crowd filled the stands.

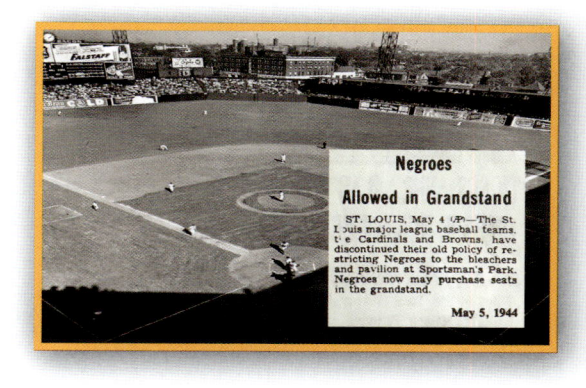

Don't think of Sportsman's Park as just a baseball stadium. Its history is long and filled with many other sports teams. It was the home field for the Saint Louis University football team as well as the NFL's All-Stars, Gunners, and Cardinals. The St. Louis Soccer League's games were played in the park during the 1930s. Soccer's National Challenge Cup tournament was played in the park in 1948. But hundreds of kids over the years made their own baseball memories in Sportsman's park. It was always a treat to play Khoury League or high school games on the home field of their baseball idols.

The Old Barn

★ ★ ★ ★ ★ ★ ★ ★ ★ ★ ★ ★ ★ ★ ★ ★ ★

The "Old Barn" on Oakland Avenue just east of Hampton Avenue hosted many legendary events in St. Louis sports history. It opened in 1929 as the permanent location for the annual National Dairy Show and soon began hosting other events to the point that it became a permanent sports venue, earning a name change to simply the Arena. The Arena, which was about the size of a 13-story building, was in the middle of a three-structure complex with smaller buildings on its east and west sides. The building on the west side housed the Arena Bowling alley.

For a short period, when Ralston Purina owned the facility and the Blues hockey team (1977–1983), the Arena was renamed the Checkerdome and painted in the company's famous red and white checkerboard square design. But what mattered was what was going on inside. The Arena hosted concerts, conventions, circuses, rodeos, and much more. More importantly, it was the home for most of the town's indoor sporting events. Hockey was one of the first to fill the stands shortly after its opening in 1929 and remained there until just before its implosion in 1999. Besides hosting basketball and soccer teams, the Arena was home to boxing, roller derby, and professional wrestling. It was the host of many of the top NCAA tournaments and saw numerous professional sports championships. If you were a sports fan in St. Louis prior to the building's demise, there had to be a time where you stepped into the "Old Barn" for an evening of unforgettable sports memories.

St. Louis Public School Stadium

★ ★ ★ ★ ★ ★ ★ ★ ★ ★ ★ ★ ★

The St. Louis Public School Stadium, located on Kingshighway Avenue just north of St. Louis Avenue, was completed in 1928. It was built to provide a centralized, multipurpose facility for the needs of the city's public schools. The stadium was regularly home to the school system's football, track & field, and volleyball events, as well as various schools' marching band events.

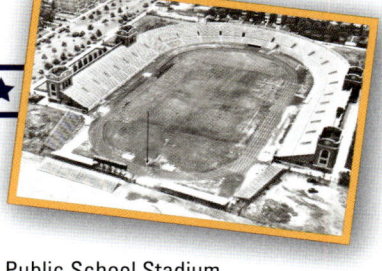

Public School Stadium
Courtesy of: Missouri History Museum, St. Louis

The stadium was also used for other sporting and city-wide events. It hosted early non-NFL football teams like the St. Louis Gunners and the St. Louis Blues. It was also the site of many important local and international soccer matches. Powerful foreign teams such as Glasgow Celtic, Liverpool, and Manchester United played there. Many St. Louisans have special memories of attending the annual Shriner's Circus and fireworks display each July.

One of the most memorable moments in American sports history took place at the stadium on June 21, 1963. In an Amateur Athletic Union (AAU) National Track & Field Championship meet, "Bullet" Bob Hayes set the world record in the 100 yard dash with a time of 9.1 seconds. Declared the fastest human in the world, Hayes would win the gold medal in the 100-meter dash in the 1964 Olympics and then become a Pro Bowl wide receiver for the Dallas Cowboys.

The stadium's demise was a product of the post–World War II urban sprawl that created new school districts outside the city limits with their own fields and complexes. The stadium was finally razed in the late 1970s, leaving special moments and memories for those who once gathered there to watch the games and events.

Index

1904 World's Fair, 82, 123, 157, 159
9/11, 128
A League of Their Own, 17
Aaron, Tommy, 129
ABA, See *American Basketball Association*.
ABC Hall of Fame, 50
Affton High School, 26
AFL, See *American Football League* or *Arena Football League*.
African American, 5, 9, 12, 34, 37, 123, 142–143, 173
Albany Firebirds, 78
Ali, Muhammad, 163–165
All American Girls Professional Baseball League, 17
Alorton, 151
Amateur Athletic Union, 175
American Association, 2, 13, 20, 172
American Basketball Association, 28, 38–39, 112
American Bowling Congress, 48, 50–51
American Collegiate Hockey Association, 92
American Express Championship, 128
American Football League, 63, 65
American Hockey Association, 82
American Hockey League, 82
American Indoor Football, 79
American Indoor Soccer Association, 116
American League, 3–4, 7, 14, 172
American Negro League, 10–11
American Professional Football Association, 60
American Underdog, 73
Anderson, Donny and Otis, 66
Angotti, Lou, 84
Angsman, Elmer, 64
Anheuser-Busch, 47, 50, 83
Annis, Bob, 101–102
Arena Bowl, 56–57
Arena Bowling Alley, 174
Arena Football League, 78
Arena Pro Football, 79
Arena, The, See *St. Louis Arena*.
Argentina, 129
Arizona Cardinals, See *St. Louis Cardinals (football)*.
Armstrong, Henry, 163
Ashe, Arthur, 132–133, 141–143, 147
Atlanta Chiefs, 105

Atlanta Hawks, See *St. Louis Hawks*.
Aucamp, Carol, See *Hanks, Carol*.
Auerbach, Red, 36
Augusta National Golf Club, 124, 129–130
Australia(n), 125, 146
Australian Open, 137, 140, 143
BAA, See *Basketball Association of America*.
Bahr, Walter, 101
Bakken, Jim, 67
Ball, Philip, 4
Ballpark Village, 55
Baltimore Bays, 105
Baltimore Blast, 118
Baltimore Colts, 70–71
Baltimore Orioles, 3
Baltimore Ravens, 71
Banks, Tom, 67
Barnes, Marvin "Bad News," 39
Baseball Hall of Fame, 5–6, 8–9, 55, 170
Baseball Writers Association of America, 170
Basketball Association of America, 31
Basketball Hall of Fame, 31–37, 35–37, 39, 43
Battle Creek Belles, 17
Bauman, Frank, 16
Baylor, 43
Beaty, Zelmo, 33
Beaumont High School, 14, 16, 29
Bell, James "Cool Papa," 1, 8–9
Belleclair, 153
Bellerive Country Club, 122–123, 125–128
Belleville, 7, 18, 129, 131, 139, 153
Bellinger, Tony, 112
Ben Millers, the, 96
Bergmann, Erma, 17–18
Berkmeyer, Barb and Skip, 131
Berra, Yogi, 14, 20
Betz, Caroline Kindle, 120
Bick, Sam, 112–113
Bidwill, Bill/Bidwell Family, 60, 65, 68, 104
Bidwill, Charles, Jr., 65
Bidwill, Charles, Sr., 64
Bidwill, Violet, 64–65, 67, 71
Billie Jean King Cup, 134
BJ's, the, 52–54
Blattner, Buddy, 169
Blaylock, Janie, 25
Bluth, Mike, 46, 49–51
Bluth, Ray, 49–51, 56
BMW, 129
Bogacki, John, Jr., 52–53
Bok, Benjamin, 157
Bommarito Automotive Group, 154

Bonetti, Peter, 108
Boone Valley, 129
Borghi, Frank, 96, 101–102
Bornhop, Leroy, 54
Boston Celtics, 33, 36–37
Boston Garden, 90
Boston Red Sox, 5
Boston University, 90
Bottomley, Jim, 14
Bowling for Dollars, 57
Bowling Green, 29
Bowling Magazine, 50
Bowling Proprietors' Association of America, 51, 55
Bowman, Scotty, 87
Boyer, Ken, 14
Bradshaw, Jay and Linda, 52–53
Brady, Tom, 73
Brazil, 102, 109
Breadon, Sam, 4
Bricka, Justina, 132–133, 145–147
Briscoe, Jack, 160
Britton, Helene, 13
Brock, Lou, 4
Brody, King Kong, 160
Broeg, Bob, 170
Bronze Boot, the, See *Joseph Carenza, Sr., Perpetual Trophy*.
Brooks, Rich, 71, 75
Brown, Mordecai "Three Finger," 6
Brown, Willard, 5, 12
Bruce, Isaac, 73
Buchholz, Earl, Jr. "Butch," 133, 137, 141
Buck, Jack, 168–169
Buckets on Deck, 54
Budweiser Bowling Team, 47, 49–52
Buffalo Bisons, See *St. Louis Hawks*.
Burlison, Roy, 23–24
Burnes, Bob, 170
Busch Family, 123
Busch Seniors, 96
Busch Stadium/Busch Stadium II, 55, 66, 68, 71, 93, 103–105, 107, 109
Bush, George H. W. and George W., 131
Bush, Homer, 16
Cahokia Downs, 151
Calcavecchia, Mark, 128
California Seals, 86
California Surf, 108
Caray, Harry, 168–169
Carlin Racing, 154
Carolina Cougars, See *Spirits of St. Louis*.
Carolina Panthers, 72
Caron, Alain, 84
Carroll College, 59
Carter, Don, 46, 49–51, 56
Carvel, Alan, 133

176 | ST. LOUIS SPORTS MEMORIES

Cary, Clayton, 29
Casals, Rosemary, 147
Casey, Pete, 61
Catholic Youth Council, 95
CBC High School, 16
CBS, 104
Centene Community Ice Center, 92
Centene Stadium, 120
Central Collegiate Hockey Association, 90–91
Central High School, 16
Central West End, 157
Cepeda, Orlando, 14
Ceresia, Don, 106
Cetwinski, Eddie, 54
Chalupny, Lori, 103, 119
Chamberlain, Wilt, 35
Championship Auto Racing Teams, 154
Chandra, Akshat, 157
Charleston, Oscar, 8–9
Charlotte Panthers, 24
Chase Park Plaza Hotel, 160–161
Checkerdome, The, See *St. Louis Arena*.
Chess Club and Scholastic Centre of St. Louis, See *Saint Louis Chess Club*.
Chess Congress, 157
Chesterfield, 71
Chicago American Giants, 9, 173
Chicago Bears, 64–65, 72
Chicago Blackhawks, 56, 84–86
Chicago Cardinals, See *St. Louis Cardinals (football)*.
Chicago Cubs, 6–7, 13, 17
Chicago Spurs, 105
Chicago Stadium, 85
Chicago Whales, 6–7
Chicago White Stockings, 13
Chi-Doy, Cheung, 106
Childress, Joe, 66
Christman, Paul, 64
Christmas, 136
Cincinnati Reds (baseball), 6
Cincinnati Reds (football), 62–63
Cincinnati Title, 146
Civil War, 2
Clay, Cassius, See *Ali, Muhammad*.
Clear, Eddie, 106
Clemens, Teri, 44–45
Clements, Dave, 113
Cleveland Crunch, 117
Cleveland High School, 29
Cleveland Indians, 5, 61
Cleveland Rams, See *St. Louis Rams*.
Cochems, Eddie, 59
Cole, Nat King, 161
Coleman, Vince, 14

Collegiate Chess National Championship, 157
Collins, Sandy, 148
Collinsville, 29, 151
Colombo, Charlie, 101–102
Comiskey Park, 162, 164
Concord Bowl, 53
Concordia Seminary, 136
Conlon, Jim, 100
Connecticut Huskies, 43
Connors, Gloria, 139
Connors, Jimmy, 133, 139–141, 143
Conrad, Bobby Joe, 66
Conzelman, Jimmy, 62
Cook, John, 126
Cooper, Chuck, 33
Cooper, Mort, 14
Cordia, John, 29
corkball, 19–21
Cornell, 90
Costas, Bob, 2, 39, 170
Counce, Dan, 113
Council, Ryan, 54
COVID, 77, 80, 120
Creve Coeur Racquet Club, 149
Crowe, John David, 66
Curtis, Peter, 147
Curtis Cup, 131
Cyclones, 2
Dallas, Don, 98
Dallas Blackhawks, 84–85
Dallas Cowboys, 66, 175
Dallas Tornado, 110
Davenport, Lindsey, 149
Davis, Dwight, 95, 133–136, 149
Davis, Russ, 57
Davis Cup, 134, 138, 143
de Vicenzo, Roberto, 129
Dean, Dizzy, 4, 11, 14, 169
Delabar, Eric, 112
Delaware Smash, 149
Demaret, Jimmy, 124
Detroit Lions, 63
Devine, Bing, 111
Dick the Bruiser, 160
Dierdorf, Dan, 66–67
Dillon, Travis, 135–136
Dobler, Conrad, 67
Doby, Larry, 5
Domino's Pizza Team Tennis League, See *World Team Tennis*.
Doral, 124
Doran, Daryl, 114, 116–118, 120
Dover Motorsports Inc., 154
Drewes, Ted, Sr., 135–136
Druhm, Connor, 54
Duke, 43
Dunn, Crystal, 94
Dwight Davis Challenge Trophy, 135–136
Dwight Davis Memorial Tennis Center, 149

Dyson, Kevin, 73
East St. Louis, 16, 139, 152, 167
East St. Louis High School, 16
East Saint Louis Jockey Club, 151
Eastern Colored League, 10
East-West League, 10
Ebert, Don, 112–113
Ebonite, 50
Edison, Thomas, 59
Edwards, Mark, 43
Edwardsville, 97–98, 100, 144
Eisel, Mary-Ann, 133, 145, 147
Ellis, Cowboy Bob, 160
England/English, 101–102, 108
Eschenbrenner, Jim, 27, 38, 82–83
Esposito, Phil, 84
Esquire, 157
Evans, Ray, 108
FAA, 128
Fahey, Nancy, 43
Fairgrounds Park, 2
Faldo, Nick, 126
Family Arena, 40, 78–79, 92, 118, 120
Fairmont Park/Fairmont Derby, 151
Farrow, Juan, 144
Faulk, Marshall, 73
Federal League, 6–7
Federko, Bernie, 92
FIFA, 103
Finnie, Roger, 67
Fischer, Pat, 67
Fisher, Jeff, 75
Flach, Ken, 133, 144
Flair, Ric, 160
Flood, Curt, 6
Florissant, 18, 24, 123
Florissant Valley Junior College/Florissant Valley Community College, See *St. Louis Community College-Florissant Valley*.
Floriss Lanes, 49
Floyd, Donna, 147
Ford Frick Award, 170
Forest Hills Country Club, 129
Forest Park, 16, 82, 123, 149
Forest Park Golf Course, 123
Foster Hewitt Memorial Award, 170
Fox Run, 129
Francis Field, 62, 107
Francois, Curtis, 154
Frankiewicz, Casey, 106
Freese, David, 14
French, 133, 157
French Open, 137, 143–144, 146
Froehling, Frank, 138
Frontiere, Georgia, 70–71, 73–74

FORGOTTEN TEAMS AND MOMENTS FROM AMERICA'S BEST SPORTS TOWN | 177

Frisch, Frankie, 14
Fuhrmann, Joe, 106
Funk, Terry, 160
Furrier, Dick, 23–24
Gaedel, Eddie, 5
Gaetjens, Joe, 101–102
Galanti, Tom, 113
Gall, David, 151
Gallagher, Jim, 126
Gallagher, Scott, 96
Game of Their Lives, The, 101
Garagiola, Joe, 56, 168–169
Garofalo, Sam, 52
Gateway Motorsports Park, See *St. Louis International Raceway*.
Gatlin, Bill, 133
Gentile, Carl, 106
Georgia Dome, 72
German(y), 105–106
Getzlow, Greg, 53–54
Giants Park, 9
Gibson, Althea, 143
Gibson, Bob, 4, 14
Glasgow Celtic, 175
Glavin, Tony, 112–113
Glen Echo Country Club, 122
Goalby, Bob, 129–131
Golden Gloves, 164
Goodin, Mike, 54
Goodwill Games, 167
Gorgeous George, 160
Grand Avenue Ball Grounds, See *Sportsman's Park*.
Grand Slam, 125, 133, 137, 140, 143–147
Granite City, 16, 153
Granite City High School, 16
Gray, Mel, x, 66, 177
Gray, Pete, 5
Great Britain, 126, 131, 146
Great Depression, 8, 10–11, 15, 83
Greeley, Horace, 108
Green, Roy, 66
Green Bay Packers, 61, 63, 67
Green Jacket, 129–130
Greer, Curtis, 67
Grimm, Tom, 53
Groom, Bob, 7
Guelker, Bob, 97–98
Guenzler, Pat, 25–26
Guerin, Richie, 33
Gutendorf, Rudy, 106
Haas, Jay, 131
Hackett, Winston, 112
Hagan, Cliff, 27, 33, 36
Hagan, Walter, 125
Hamm, Mia, 94
Hammond Pros, 61
Handlan's Park Grounds, 6
Hanheide, George, 112
Hankemeyer, Jim, 54
Hanks, Carol, 133, 145–147
Hanks, Tom, 17
Hannum, Alex, 33

Harder, Pat, 64
Harmon, Claude, 125
Harrawood Complex, 26
Harrisburg Heat, 117
Harrisburg Stars, 11–12
Harris-Stowe University/ Harris-Stowe State College, 9, 103
Hart, Jim, 66
Harvest Lanes, 54
Haslett, Jim, 75
Hatch, Morgan, 57
Hawatmeh, Abraham, 116
Hayes, Bob "Bullet," vi, 175
Heisman Trophy, 94
Henderson, Cindy, 25
Hennessey, Tom, 49, 51
Hermann, Bob, 104
Hermann Trophy, 93–94
Hermann Undertakers/ Hermanns, 49, 52
Hernandez, Keith, 14
Hickey, Eddie, 29–30
Highlands Golf and Tennis Center, See *St. Louis Amateur Athletic Association*.
Hill, the, 54, 101–102
Hoffman, Barb, 18
Hogan, Ben, 124–125
Holmes, Larry, 165
Holmes, Ray, 52
Holt, Torry, 73
Holzman, Red, 32–33
Homestead Grays, 8
Hood, Mark, 53
Hornsby, Rogers, 4, 13–14
Houston Mavericks, See *Spirits of St. Louis*.
Howard, Elston and Ryan, 14
Hudlin, Richard, 132–133, 142–143
Hudson, Bill, 58, 67, 76, 129
Hudson, Richard, 58, 67
Hull, Brett, 88
Hummel, Rick, 170
Hummers Park, 26
Hundelt, Kevin, 117–118
Hurst Bowling Supplies, 52
Ice Capades, 36
Ilijevski, Slobo, 112–114
Indianapolis ABCs, 11–12
Indianapolis Colts, 71
Indianapolis Hoosiers, 6
Indy Lights Series, 154
IndyCar, 153–154
International Basketball League, 40
International Bowling Campus, 55
International Bowling Museum and Hall of Fame, 48, 55
International Olympic Committee, 156
International Tennis Hall of Fame, 137–138, 140, 143

International Women's Professional Softball Assocation, 25
Iowa Barnstormers, 78
Ireland/Irish, 30, 131, 147
Irsay, Robert, 70
Irwin, Hale, 129–130
Jackman, Barrett, 92
Jeffrey, Bill, 101–102
Jennings, Bill, 112
Jennings High School, 16
John, Emilio, 91
John Burroughs High School, 130, 146
Johnson, Charlie, 66
Johnson, Dwayne "the Rock," 77
Johnson, Ryan, 92
Johnson, Walter, 142
Jolson, Al, 163
Jones, Mike, 73
Joplin, 130
Jordan, Kathy, 144
Jordan, Michael, 114
Joseph Carenza, Sr., Perpetual Trophy, 103
Joyce, Joan, 25
Joyner-Kersee, Jackie, 166–167
Kalicanin, Mike, 106
Kansas City Blues, 63
Kansas City Comets, 120
Kansas City Monarchs, 8, 11, 173
Karl, Jeff, 100
Kastner, Jeff, 156
KDNL-TV, 26, 57
Kehoe, Bob, 107
Kelly, Dan, 89, 170
Kelly, John, 170
Kennedy, Jaqueline, 167
Kennedy, John F., 164
Kennedy, Lindsay, 103
Kennedy Stadium, 24
Kensingtons, The, 96
Kent, Richard, 9
Kentucky Colonels, 39
Keough, Harry, 97, 99, 101–102
Keough, Ty, 112
Kevlishvilli, Robby, 157
Khorassan Room, 161
Khoury, Dorothy and George, 15–16
Khoury League, 15–16, 173
Kiel Auditorium/Kiel Center, 32–34, 92, 116–117, 160
Kinealy, Jack, 106
King, Billie Jean, 25, 134, 146–147
KIRL, 152
Kissel, Audrey "Kiss," 18
Klitschko, Vitali and Wladimir, 165
KMOX, 39, 170
Kolbl, Rudi, 105–106
Koch Park, 24

Koepka, Brooks, 125–127
Koplar, Harold, 160
Korean War, 20, 102
Kournikova, Anna, 149
KPLR-TV, 16, 158, 160–161
Kraehe, Ollie, 61
Krat, Nick, 106
Kroenke, Stan, 73–74
KTVI-TV, 57
Kuharich, Joe, 65
Kutis, 96
KXOK, 152
Kyle, Gus, 84, 88
Ladue, 123
Ladue High School, 147
Lafayette High School, 14
Lake Hill Speedway, 153
Landis, Kenesaw Mountain, 7
Lane, McArthur, 66
Laux, France, 169
Laver, Rod, 138
Lawn Tennis Challenge, 134
Leach, Rich, 144
Lehman, Louis, 29
Lessman, Ric, 16–17
Lewis & Clark Community College, 100
LFL, See *Lingerie Football League.*
Lightfoot, Randy, 54
Lindbergh, Charles, 38
Lindenwood University, 53, 80, 92
Linehan, Scott, 75
Lingerie Football League, 79
Liston, Sonny, 162–165
Liverpool, 175
Loeffler, Ken, 31
Logan, Johnny, 27, 31
Lombardi Trophy, 74
Lombardo-Baker, Karen, 99–100
Londoff, Johnny, 129
Long Beach Grand Prix, 153
Los Angeles Dodgers, 13–14
Los Angeles Kings, 86
Los Angeles Lazers, 114
Los Angeles Raiders, See *Oakland Raiders.*
Los Angeles Rams, See *St. Louis Rams.*
Los Angeles Toros, 105
Lovellette, Clyde, 33
LPGA, 25, 123, 129–130
Lucas, Maurice, 39
Luden, Jana and Jim, 52–53
Luenemann, Rich, 45
Lyons, Chubby, 101
Maca, Joe, 101
Macauley, Ed, 29–31, 33, 36–37
Mackey, James "Biz," 8
Madison, 154
Madison Square Garden, 29
Madonna, 17
Major Arena Soccer League, 120

Major Indoor Soccer League, 103, 111–116, 118, 120
Major League Softball, 23, 25
Maki, Wayne, 84
Makowski, Greg, 112
Malone, Moses, 27, 39
Manchester United, 175
Mandaric, Milan, 114–116
Maplewood, 48
Marandi, Cemil Can Ali, 157
Marciano, Rocky, 165
Marion, Marty, 14, 18
Markwort Sporting Goods, 21
Martin, Dean, 161
Martin, Slater, 33
Martz, Mike, 73, 75
Maryland Heights, 92
Masters, the, 129–131
Masters League, 50
Mattke, John, 148
Maxvill, Dal, 16
Mayers, Jamal, 92
Mays, Willie, 113
McBride, Bake, 14
McBride, Pat, 106–108, 112–113
McCarver, Tim, 169
McCluer North High School, 26
McDermott, Bill, 170
McDonnell, Dan, 112
McEnroe, John, 149
McGee, Willie, 14
McIlvenny, Ed, 101
McKendree College Bearcats, 57
McKinley, Chuck, 133, 138
McLaughlin, Dan, 169
McMahon, Vince, 76, 161
Medwick, Joe "Ducky," 4, 14
Meinert, Dale, 67
Meinert, Wayne, 152–153
Memphis State, 41
Meramec Community College, 16, 26, 100
Meramec River, 26
Meyers, Rita "Slats," 18
Michelob Light, 129
Mid-America Raceway, 152–153
Middleman, Steve, 106
Miller, Brad, 54
Miller, Larry, 133
Mills, Charles, 9
Milwaukee Badgers, 61
Milwaukee Brewers, 3
Milwaukee Hawks, See *St. Louis Hawks.*
Milwaukee Wave, 117
Minneapolis Millerettes, 18
Minnesota North Stars, 86–87
Minnesota Vikings, 72
MISL, See *Major Indoor Soccer League.*
Mississippi River, 48, 97, 122, 139, 144, 151, 153

Missouri Athletic Club, 94
Missouri History Museum, 1, 8–10, 13, 93, 107, 109, 111, 116, 142, 158, 160, 175
Missouri Monsters, 79
Missouri National Guard, 62, 141
Missouri River Otters, 92
Missouri State High School, 45
Missouri State Senior, 131
Missouri Valley Conference, 29
Missouri Women's Amateur, 131
Mitchell, Stump, 66
Mobile Gulls, 24
Molina, Yadier, 4
Monday Night Miracle, 88
Montreal Canadians, 87
Montreal Maroons, 83
Montreal Royals, 24
Moon, Wally, 14
Moor, Terry, 148
Moore, Terry, 56
Morgan Athletic Club, 64
Morning Stars, 2
Mortimer, Angela, 146
Moscow Red Army team, 110
Moser, Mark, 117–118
Muchnick, Sam, 159–161
Muhammad, Eddie Mustafa, 165
Mullins, Patrick, 94
Muny Leagues, 95
Muny Tennis Association, 143
Musial, Stan, 1, 4, 14, 56, 85, 111
Muskegon Lassies, 17
NAACP, 164
Nagel, Kel, 125
Naismith Memorial Basketball Hall of Fame, 28
NASCAR, 153–154
Nastase, Ilie, 140
National Amateur Cup, 95–97
National Basketball Association, ix, 13, 27–28, 32–40
National Challenge Cup, 96–97, 100
National Clay Court Championship, 146
National Dairy Show, 174
National Football League, 60–67, 70–74, 76, 78, 104, 173, 175
National Hockey League, 56, 81–86, 88–90, 92, 112
National Hot Rod Association, 153–154
National Indoor Football League, 78–79
National Invitational Tournament, 29
National Junior College Athletic Association, 99–100

National League, 2–4, 6, 13, 172
National Muny Recreation Federation, 135
National Parks, 133
National Professional Soccer League, 104–105, 116
National Register of Historic Places, 48
National Women's Football Association, 80
National Wrestling Alliance, 160
Nationwide Series, 154
NBA, See *National Basketball Association*.
NBA World Championship, 37
NCAA, 29, 41–43, 45, 57, 76, 90, 92, 94, 97–99, 103, 138–139, 143–144, 170, 174
Negro American League, 11
Negro National League, 8–12, 173
Negro Southern League, 10–11
Nelson, David, 59
Nelson, Nancy "Boomer," 25
Newman, Paul, 152
New Orleans Saints, 72
New Orleans Stars, 11–12
New York Arrows, 112, 114
New York Cosmos, 107, 109
New York Generals, 105
New York Giants, 68, 113
New York Guardians, 77
New York Knicks, 33
New York Nets, 39
New York Times, The, 102
New York University, 30, 45
New York Yankees, 2, 13, 113
NFL, See *National Football League*.
NFL Hall of Fame, 59, 62, 66
NHL, See *National Hockey League*.
NHL Hall of Fame, 84, 87, 89
NHRA, See *National Hot Rod Association*.
Nicklaus, Jack, 125–126, 129
Noffke, Rich, 28, 79, 93
Norman K. Probstein Golf Course, See *Forest Park Golf Course*.
Normandie Golf Club, 122
Normandy High School, 29
Norris, James, 84–86
North American Soccer League, 106–107, 110
North Dakota Fighting Sioux, 90
North Korea, 102
North Side, 20, 49, 95, 172
Norwood Hills Country Club, 122, 124
Oakland Clippers, 105
Oakland Raiders, 71
Oates, Adam, 88
O'Connor, Pat, 160

O'Farrell, Bob, 14
O'Hara, Johnny, 169
Ohio State Buckeyes, 90
Old Warson Country Club, 123, 125
Olympics, 97, 119, 122, 134, 144, 156, 158–159, 164–165, 167, 170, 175
Ootes, Lennart, 156–157
Oorang Indians, 61
Orange Bowl, 67
Orhan, Yilmaz, 112
Ornest, Harry, 148–149
Ossola, Joe, 29
O. T. Hill, 54
Otis, Jim, 66
Pacific High School, 26
Paige, Satchel, 1, 11, 173
Palmer, Arnold, 126, 129
Pan American Games, 167
Pang, Kelly, 44
Pariani, Gino, 101–102
Parks, E. J., 54
Parkway Central Senior High School, 71
Patrick, Lynn, 87
Patterson, Floyd, 162, 164
Patterson, Pat, 49, 51
PBA, See *Professional Bowlers Association*.
PBA Hall of Fame, 50–51, 54–55
Pebble Beach, 124
Pecher, Steve, 112–113
Pele, 109
Penn State, 102
Pentagon, the, 128
Peoria Redwings, 18
Peroni, Alex, 154
Pettit, Bob, 13, 27, 32–33, 35, 37
PGA, 124–127, 129–131
Philadelphia Flyers, 86–87
Philadelphia Patriots, 24
Philadelphia Phillies, 14
Philadelphia Spartans, 105
Philadelphia Warriors, 31
Phillips, Dave, 16
Pittsburgh Penguins, 86
Pittsburgh Phantoms, 105
Pittsburgh Pirates, 63
Plank, Eddie, 7
Player, Gary, 125
Pogrzeba, Norb, 106
Polish, 107
Pook, Chris, 153–154
Popovic, Don, 114–115
Port, Ellen, 130–131
President's Cup (chess), 157
Presidents Cup (golf), 127
Price, Bill, 133
Price, Nick, 126
Price, Sandra, 146
Pro Bowl, 175
Pro Bowl West, 52
Professional Bowlers Association, 50–51

Prohibition, 47
Pujols, Albert, 4, 14
Puls, Joe, 106
Queen Elizabeth, 132
Quillman, Clem, 23–24
Racine Belles, 17–18
Radosavljevic, Predrag, 114
Raft, George, 163
Ralston, John, 138
Ralston Purina, 88, 91, 174
Ramirez, Alejandro, 157
Randall, Rick, 141
Randle, Sonny, 66
Rankin, Judy, 123, 130
Rawlings, 21
Raymonds, Henry, 29
Redbird Lanes, 56
Redloff, John, 24
Reeves, Dan, 70
Reynolds, Candy, 148
Richmond Heights, 142
Rickey, Branch, 3–4, 7
River City Raiders, 79
RiverCity Renegades, 78
Roach, John, 66
Robertson, Oscar, 35
Robinson, Bradbury, 59
Robinson, Jackie, 5, 12
Robison, Helene, See *Helene Britton*.
Robison Field, 14, 172
Rochester Royals, 36
Roddick, Andy, 149
Rodgers, Buddy, 159
Roland, Johnny, 66
Romero, Emilio, 112
Rooney, John, 169
Rooney, Tim, 112
Rose, Carl, 112
Rosenbloom, Carroll, 70–71
Rubinoff, Ed, 146
Russell, Bill, 33, 35–37
Russia(n), 110
Ruth, Babe, 113
Ryder Cup, 125–126
St. Charles, 40, 53–54, 78–79, 92
St. Louis Aces, 148–149
St. Louis All-Stars, 60–63
St. Louis Amateur Athletic Association, 123
St. Louis Ambush, 116–118, 120
St. Louis Archdiocese, 95
St. Louis Archers, 119
St. Louis Arena, 28, 31, 39, 41–42, 56–57, 82–88, 90–92, 110–111, 114–116, 148, 160, 174
St. Louis Armory, 133, 141, 143
St. Louis Athletica, 103, 119
St. Louis Baseball Cardinals Hall of Fame, 55
St. Louis BattleHawks, 76–77
St. Louis Blues (football), 63

180 | ST. LOUIS SPORTS MEMORIES

St. Louis Blues (hockey), 33, 82, 84–92, 112, 117, 148, 170, 174–175
St. Louis Bombers, 27, 31–32, 36
St. Louis Braves, 84–85
St. Louis Browns (baseball), 1, 3–5, 7, 9, 12–14, 16, 26, 86, 112, 149, 171–173, 177
St. Louis Browns (softball), 22–24
St. Louis Brown Stockings, 2, 13, 20, 172
St. Louis Budweisers, See *Budweiser Bowling Team.*
St. Louis Cardinals (baseball), 2–7, 9–10, 13–14, 16, 33, 55, 64, 71, 86–87, 113, 159–160, 172–173, 177
St. Louis Cardinals (football), 33, 60, 64–69, 72, 104, 141
Saint Louis Chess Club, 156–157
St. Louis City SC, 94, 120
St. Louis Community College–Florissant Valley, 97, 99–100
St. Louis Community College–Forest Park, 100
St. Louis Community College–Meramec, See *Meramec Community College.*
St. Louis Country Club, 121, 124
St. Louis Eagles, 83
St. Louis Flyers, 82–83
St. Louis Giants, 8–9, 12
St. Louis Globe-Democrat, 170
St. Louis Gunners, 60, 62–64, 173, 175
St. Louis Hawks, 13, 28, 31–38, 68
St. Louis Hinder Club, 141
St. Louis Hummers, 25–26
St. Louis International Raceway, 152–154
St. Louis Magazine, 141
St. Louis Maroons, 2
St. Louis Media Museum, 168, 170
St. Louis Perfectos, 3
St. Louis Post-Dispatch, 16, 26
St. Louis Public School Stadium, 62, 175
St. Louis Raiders, 96
St. Louis Rams, 60, 63, 65, 70–75, 78
St. Louis Saints, 79
St. Louis Slam, 80
St. Louis Slims, 148–149
St. Louis Soccer Park, 119
St. Louis Sports Hall of Fame, 151
St. Louis Stampede, 78
St. Louis Stars (baseball), 8–12
St. Louis Stars (soccer), 33, 104–110, 113, 170

St. Louis Steamers, 103, 111–114, 118
St. Louis Storm, 114–116
St. Louis Strikers, 119
St. Louis Swarm, 40
St. Louis Terriers, 1, 6–7
Saint Louis University, 6, 29–31, 36, 59, 90–92, 97–100, 103, 157, 173
Saint Louis University Billikens, 29–30, 90, 92
St. Louis University High School, 29
St. Louis Vipers, 92
St. Matthew's Parish, 95
St. Patrick's Day, 30, 88
St. Peters, 54
Salvador, Bryce, 92
Sampras, Pete, 149
San Diego Sockers, 114–115
San Francisco Giants, See *New York Giants.*
San Francisco Warriors, 34
Saratoga Lanes, 48, 56
Sarazen, Gene, 125
Sauers, Gene, 126
Schatzman, Marvin, 29
Schmidt, Bob and Joe, 29
Schneider, Jack, 59
Schneider, Katie Muchnick, 159, 161
Schneider, Vicki, 25–26
Schucart, Tom, 53–54
Schuurman, Renee, 146
Schwartz, Manny, 112
Scottish, 122
Scullin Steel, 96
Seguso, Robert, 144
Selman, Bill, 90–91
Sendobry, Jeff, 112
Sennwald, Charlene, 26
Serbia(n), 114
Sergota, Branko, 115
Sewell, John, 108
Shannon, Mike, 16, 169
Shelter Insurance Team, 53
Shepard, Samuel, 9
Show-Me Believers, 79
Show Me Lanes, 52
Sievers, Roy, 14
Silna, Daniel and Ozzie, 39–40
Simpkins-Ford, 96
Sinatra, Frank, 161
Sinquefield Cup, 157
Sinquefield, Rex, 156–157
Sisler, George, 1, 4, 13
SIUE, See *Southern Illinois University.*
SLU, See *Saint Louis University.*
Smith, Jackie, 66
Smith, Margaret, 132, 145
Smith, Ozzie, 4, 169
Snead, Sam, 124–125
Soldan High School, 29
Solo, Hope, 119
Solomon, Sid, Jr., 85–87, 91

Sorber, Pete, 99
Sorenstam, Annika, 129
South Africa(n), 125, 146
South Bend Blue Sox, 18
South Korea, 102
Southern Illinois University, 96–100, 103, 119, 144
Souza, Ed and John, 101
Spagnuolo, Steve, 75
Spink, J. G. Taylor, 170
Spinks, Cory, 165
Spinks, Leon, 163, 165
Spinks, Michael, 162–163, 165
Spirits of St. Louis, 27, 38–40, 170
Sports Car Club of America, 152–153
Sports Illustrated, 167
Sports Open Line, 170
Sportsman's Park, 3–4, 16, 61–63, 66, 68, 96, 171–173
Springfield Sallies, 17
Stanfield, Fred, 84
Stanford University, 43, 146
Stanley Cup (Finals), 33, 82, 86–87, 89
Stapleton, Pat, 84
Stars Park, 9
Steinmeyer, Robert, 157
Stix, Baer & Fuller, 96
Stremlau, John, 112
Stockton, J. Roy, 170
Sullivan, Steve, 112
Sumner High School, 142
Sunset Country Club, 123
Super Bowl, 70, 72–74
Susman, Karen, 146
Suttles, George "Mule," 8, 10
Sweeney, Dennis, 48
Swiercz, Dariusz, 157
Taff, Fred, 52
Tampa Bay Buccaneers, 72
Taylor, Jim "Candy," 9
Tennessee Titans, 72–73
Testa, Ron, 53–54
Thesz, Lou, 160
Thodorou, Nikolas, 157
Thompson, Bertha, 139
Thompson, Hank, 5, 12
Thorn, Rod, 33, 39
Thurmer, Steve, 22–23, 60, 62, 78
Tilley, Pat, 66
Tobin, Johnny, 7
Tom Packs Promotions, 159
Toronto Falcons, 105, 110
Torre, Joe, 14
Torrey Pines, 124
Toth, Zoltan, 115
Town and Country, 123
Trent, Ted, 10
Trevino, Lee, 126, 129
Tri-Cities Blackhawks, See *St. Louis Hawks.*
Trinity University, 138
Triple Crown (baseball), 4

FORGOTTEN TEAMS AND MOMENTS FROM AMERICA'S BEST SPORTS TOWN | 181

Triple Crown (racing), 151
Trippi, Charley, 64
Trost, Al, 108, 113
Trouppe, Quincy, 10
Truman, Harry S, 102
Tulsa Ambush, See *St. Louis Ambush.*
Turbull, Perry, 92
Turnesa, Mike, 124
Tyson, Mike, 165
UCLA, 41, 43, 139, 143, 167
Ukrainian, 159, 165
Ultimate Indoor Football League, 79
Umfleet, Bob, 25
UMSL (Rivermen/Riverwomen), See *University of Missouri.*
Unitas, Johnny, 70
United Hockey League, 92
United Soccer Association, 106
United Soccer League, 119
United States Congress, 156
United States Golf Association, 131
University City, 123
University City High School, 145
University of California, 45
University of Chicago, 142
University of Illinois, 43
University of Missouri, 98, 103, 123
Ursuline Academy, 26
US Interscholastic Tournament, 143
US Open, 51, 95–96, 121, 124–126, 129–131, 133–134, 137, 140, 143–144, 146–147
USBC, 51–52, 55
USBC Hall of Fame, 51
Usiyan, Thompson, 114–115
Vachier-Lagrave, Maxime, 157
Valley Park, 26, 153
Vaninger, Denny, 110, 112
Vashon High School, 163
Veeck, Bill, 9
Vermeil, Dick, 72–75
Vidinic, Barney, 106
Villa, Greg, 112
Virdon, Bill, 14
Vitt, Joe, 75

Von der Ahe, Chris, 2–3, 13, 20
Vowell, Larry, 23–24
Wainwright, Adam, 4
Walker, George Herbert, 121, 131
Walker Cup, 131
Wallace, Frank "Pee Wee," 101–102
Walsh, Chile, 63
Walton, Bill, 41–42
Ward, Terry, 140
Warner, Kurt, 72–74, 78
Washington University, 26, 34, 43, 45, 62, 100, 107, 131
Washington University Lady Bears, 43, 45
Weaver, Earl, 16
Weber, Dick, 49–51, 54, 56
Weber, John, 54
Weber, Pete, 51
Weeghman, Charles, 7
Wehrli, Roger, 66–67
Weidiner, Mary, 106
Wells, Linda, 25–26
Wells, Willie, 8, 10
Wentzville, 152
Western Kentucky, 29
Wheatley, Bob, 164
Whitworth, Kathy, 129
Wiestal, Kay, 106
Wightman Cup, 146
Wilcutt, D. C., 29
Wilkens, Lenny, 33
Williams, Serena and Venus, 149
Wills, Bob, 52
Wilson, Buzz, 52
Wilson, Jim, 93–94
Wilson, Larry, 66–67
Wimbledon, 133–134, 137–138, 140, 143–144, 146–147
Winter Garden Ice Rink, 82
Wirtz, Arthur, 84–86
Wirtz Family, 56
Wolfner, Violet Bidwell, See *Bidwell, Violet.*
Wolfner, Walter, 65
Women's Basketball Hall of Fame, 43
Women's Football Alliance, 80

Women's Football Association, 80
Women's International Bowling Congress, 48
Women's Professional Soccer League, 103, 119
Woods, Tiger, 125, 127–128
World Championship Tennis, 137, 143
World Chess Championship, 156
World Chess Hall of Fame, 156–157
World Cup, 97, 101–103, 119, 134, 170
World Golf Championship, 128
World Golf Hall of Fame, 130
World Indoor Soccer League, 118
World Series, 3–4, 14, 24, 26, 86, 173
World Team Tennis, 148
World Team Tennis League, 149
World Tennis League, 133
World War II, 11, 16–18, 20, 82, 96, 175
World Wide Technology Raceway at Gateway, See *St. Louis International Raceway.*
World Wrestling Entertainment, 76, 161
World's Fair, See *1904 World's Fair.*
Worrell, Todd, 14
Worsham, Lew, 121, 124
Wrape, Jack, 29
Wrenger, Willi, 106
Wrestling at the Chase, 160–161
Wright Brothers, 59
Wright, Margie, 25
Wrigley, Philip K., 17
WWE, See *World Wrestling Entertainment.*
XFL, 76
X-League Indoor Football, 79
Yeomans, Linda, 146
Young, Bob, 67
Yugoslavia, 104, 114
Zimbabwe, 126
Zungul, Steve, 112